Luna

Amazing Agent Luna

VOLUME 001

art by Shiei

story by Nunzio DeFilippis
and Christina Weir

[CONFIDENTIAL]

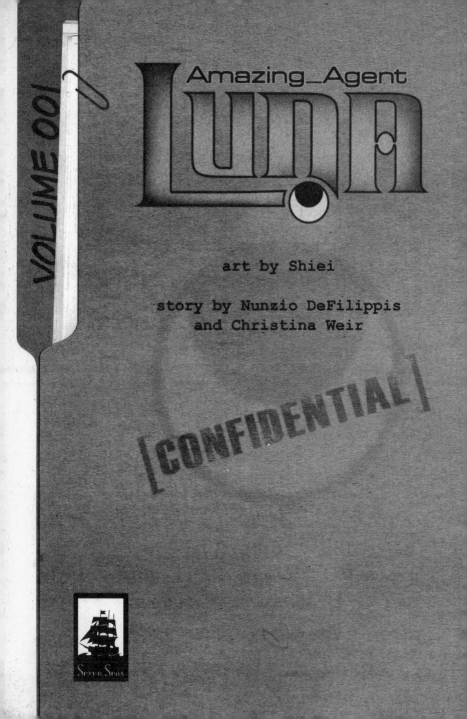

AMAZING AGENT LUNA
VOLUME 1

Staff Credits:

Art: Carmela "Shiei" Doneza

Story: Nunzio DeFilippis & Christina Weir

Tones: Jay Jimenez

Background Assists: Roland Amago

Letters: Michael David

Cover and Layout Design: Culture Crash

Editor: Jason DeAngelis

Publisher: Seven Seas Entertainment

This is a work of fiction. Names, characters, places, and incidents are the products of the author's imagination or are used fictitiously. Any resemblance to actual events, locales, or persons, living or dead, is entirely coincidental.

Visit us online at www.gomanga.com.

ISBN 1-933164-00-X

Printed in Canada

First printing: February, 2005

10 9 8 7 6 5 4 3 2 1

NEW WORLDS AT YOUR FINGERTIPS
www.gomanga.com

AMAZING AGENT LUNA - VOLUME 1

File 01
AMAZING AGENT

HE'S IN PARIS FOR SOME BUSINESS.

AMBASSADE DE BRUCKEN

BRUCKENSTEIN EMBASSY

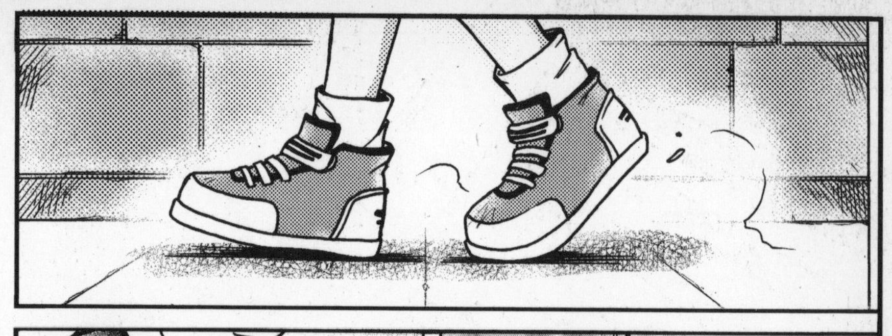

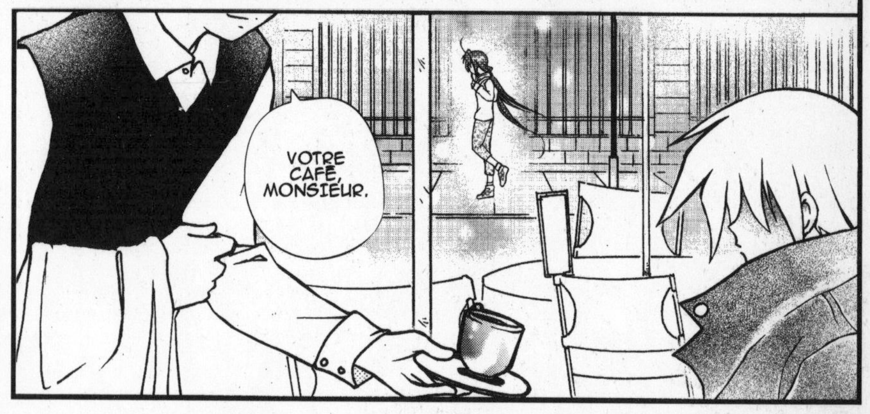
VOTRE CAFÉ, MONSIEUR.

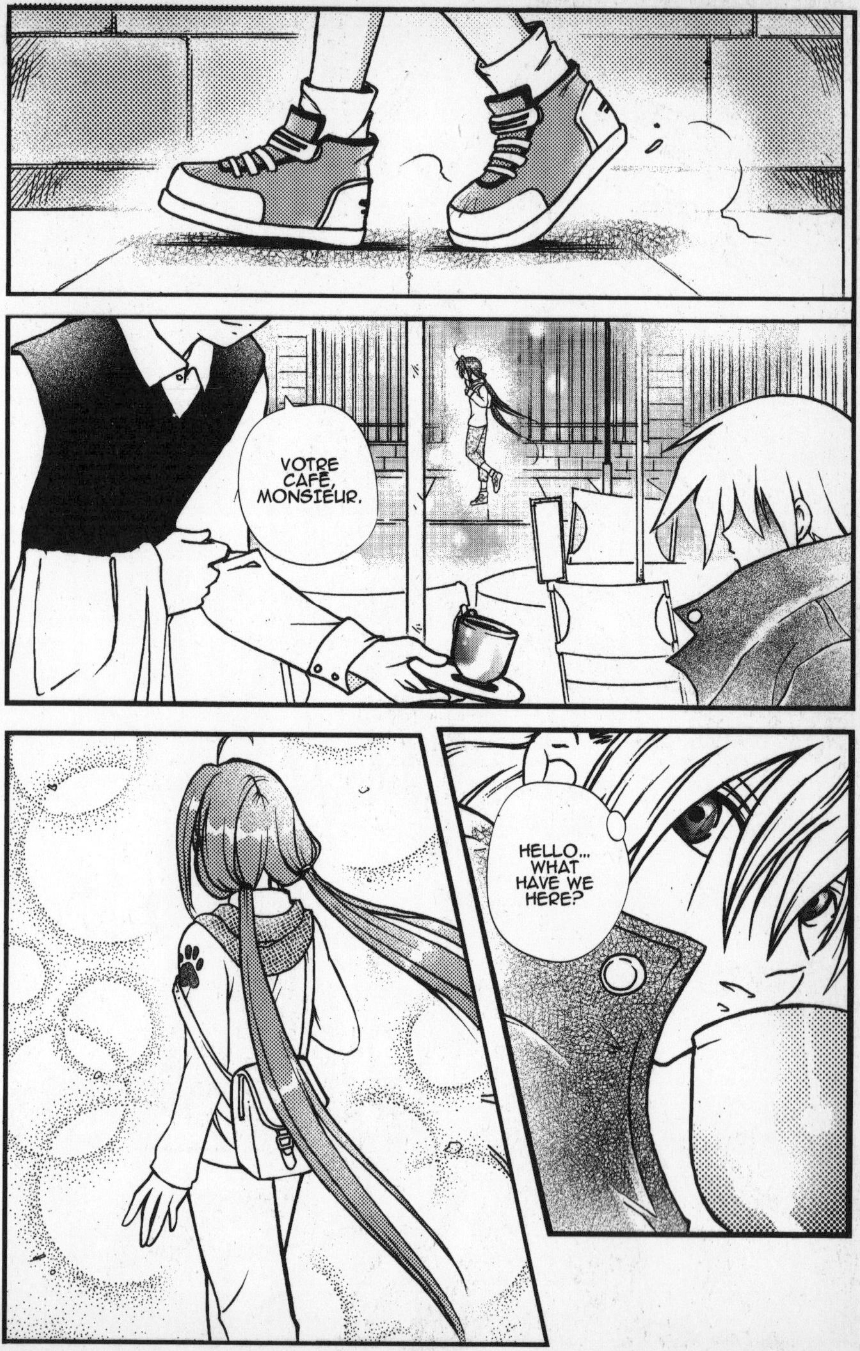

HELLO... WHAT HAVE WE HERE?

SHE DOESN'T LOOK LIKE EMBASSY STAFF...
...AND NOT FRENCH. AMERICAN MAYBE?
I'M INTRIGUED.
VERY INTRIGUED.

L'AMBASSADE DE BRUCKENSTEIN
BRUCKENSTEIN EMBASSY
THERE WE GO...
I THINK I CAUGHT HER EYE.
MAYBE SHE'LL JOIN ME FOR SOME COFFEE...
...OR NOT.

I'LL JUST TAKE MATTERS INTO MY OWN HANDS.
SHE MUST NOT HAVE SEEN ME AFTER ALL.
WELL, *THAT'S* NEVER HAPPENED BEFORE.
WHY WOULD SHE GO INTO A DEAD END ALLEY?
BECAUSE I REALLY *HAVE* TO MEET THIS GIRL.

OKAY... THIS IS ODD.

UNLESS SHE WANTED OUR FIRST MEETING TO BE IN PRIVATE.

DID I IMAGINE HER?

OH WELL... THERE ARE MANY GIRLS IN PARIS...

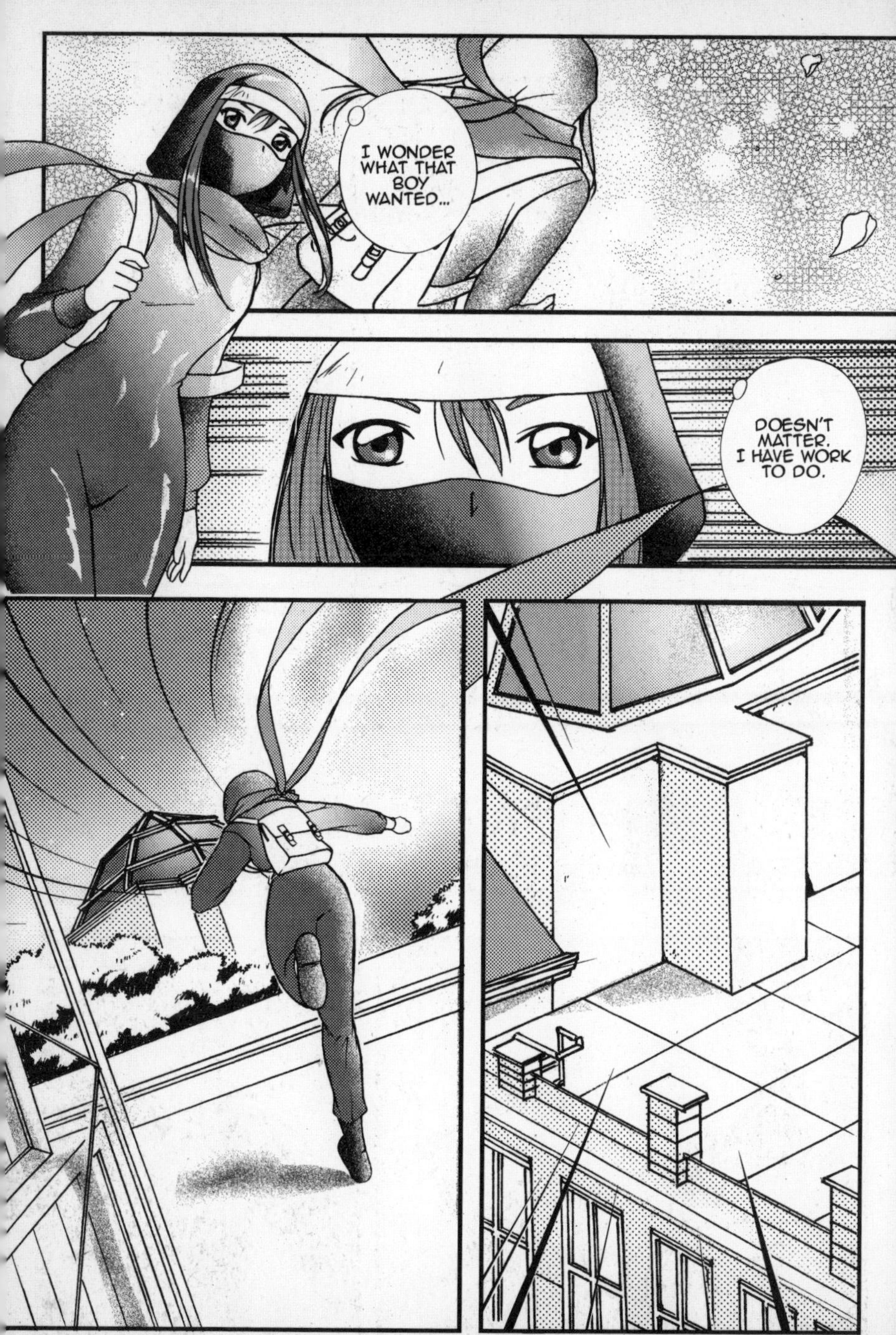
I WONDER WHAT THAT BOY WANTED...
DOESN'T MATTER. I HAVE WORK TO DO.

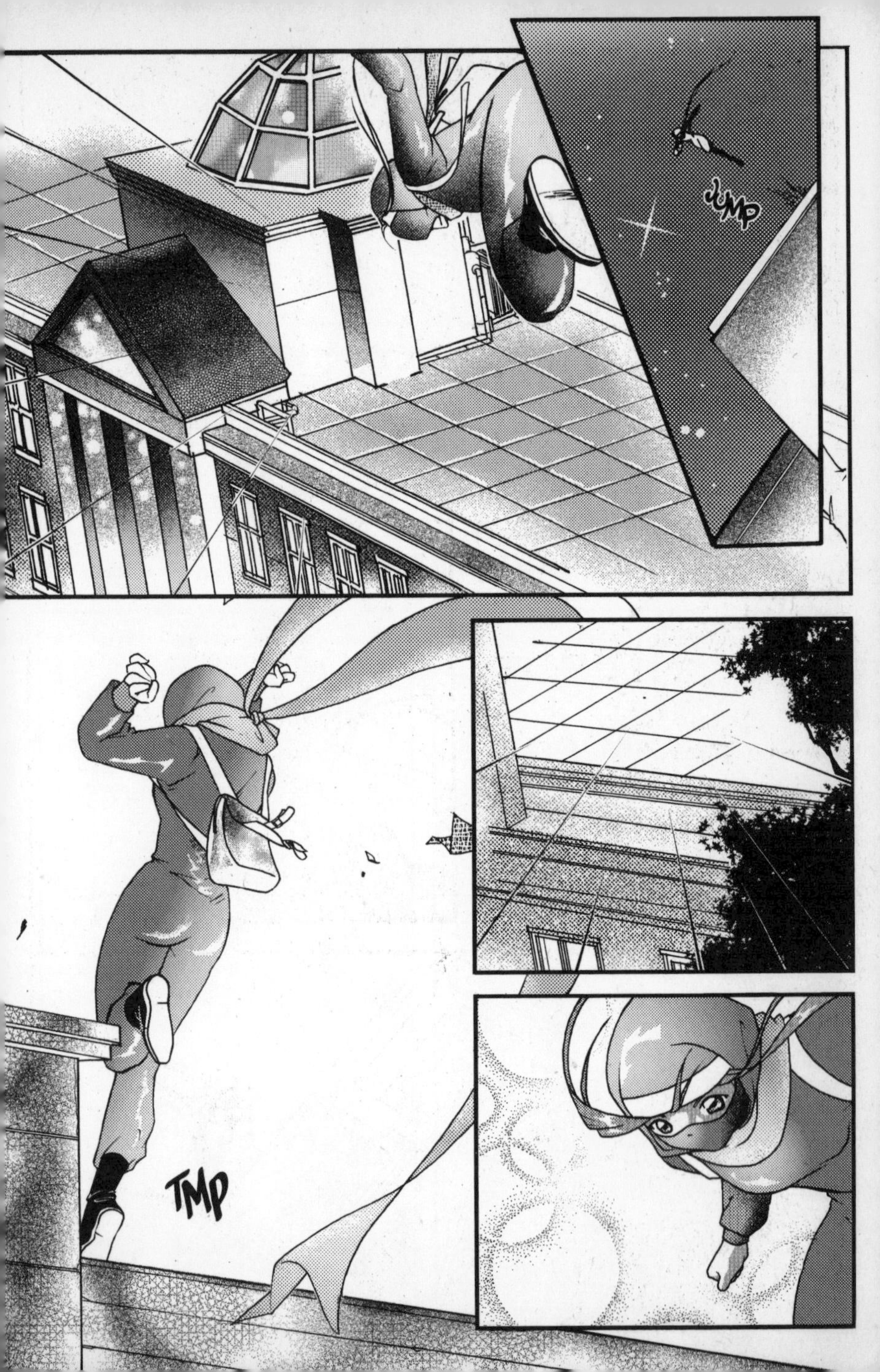
JUMP
TMP

SO FAR,
SO GOOD.

NOBODY'S
NOTICED
ME.

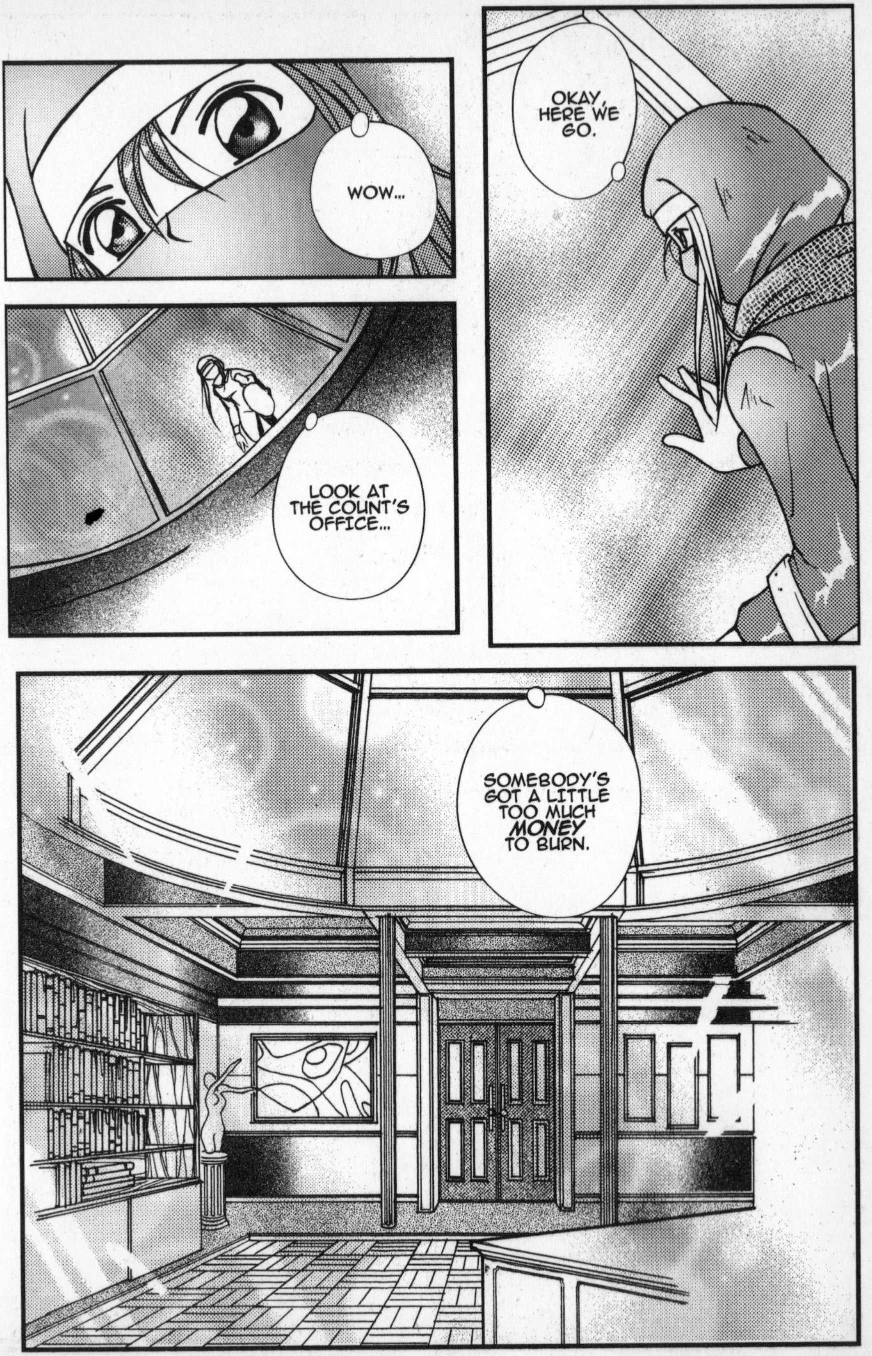

SOMEBODY'S GOT A LITTLE TOO MUCH *MONEY* TO BURN.

SCRATCH
NOW LET'S SEE WHY THE COUNT'S IN PARIS.
TURN TURN
CREAK

<WELCOME TO MY HUMBLE OFFICE, DOCTOR.>
<THANK YOU.>
<HERE WE CAN TALK IN PRIVATE.>

<HUMBLE OFFICE, INDEED.>

<ARE YOU INTERESTED IN HELPING ME WITH PROJECT SCION?>

<COUNT VON BRUCKEN, I WOULD LIKE NOTHING MORE THAN TO HELP YOU.>
<FOR THE USUAL FEE.>

<EXCELLENT.>

<THEN YOU WILL NEED TO LOOK OVER THESE FILES.>
<I WILL NEED TO BE PAID FIRST. AND I HAVE OTHER JOBS TO ATTEND TO.>
<IF I INCREASE YOUR FEE, WILL YOU PUT THIS OTHER WORK ASIDE?>
<AFTER ALL, WHO WOULD TURN DOWN A CHANCE TO WORK FOR COUNT HEINRICH VON BRUCKEN?>
<PERHAPS.>

<THEN LET US GO SEE ABOUT GETTING YOU A RETAINER...>

<...SO YOU CAN START WORK *IMMEDIATELY*.>

I WONDER WHO THAT *OTHER* MAN WAS WITH THE COUNT?

I SHOULD PROBABLY WAIT TIL THE COAST IS *CLEAR*.

SLAM!

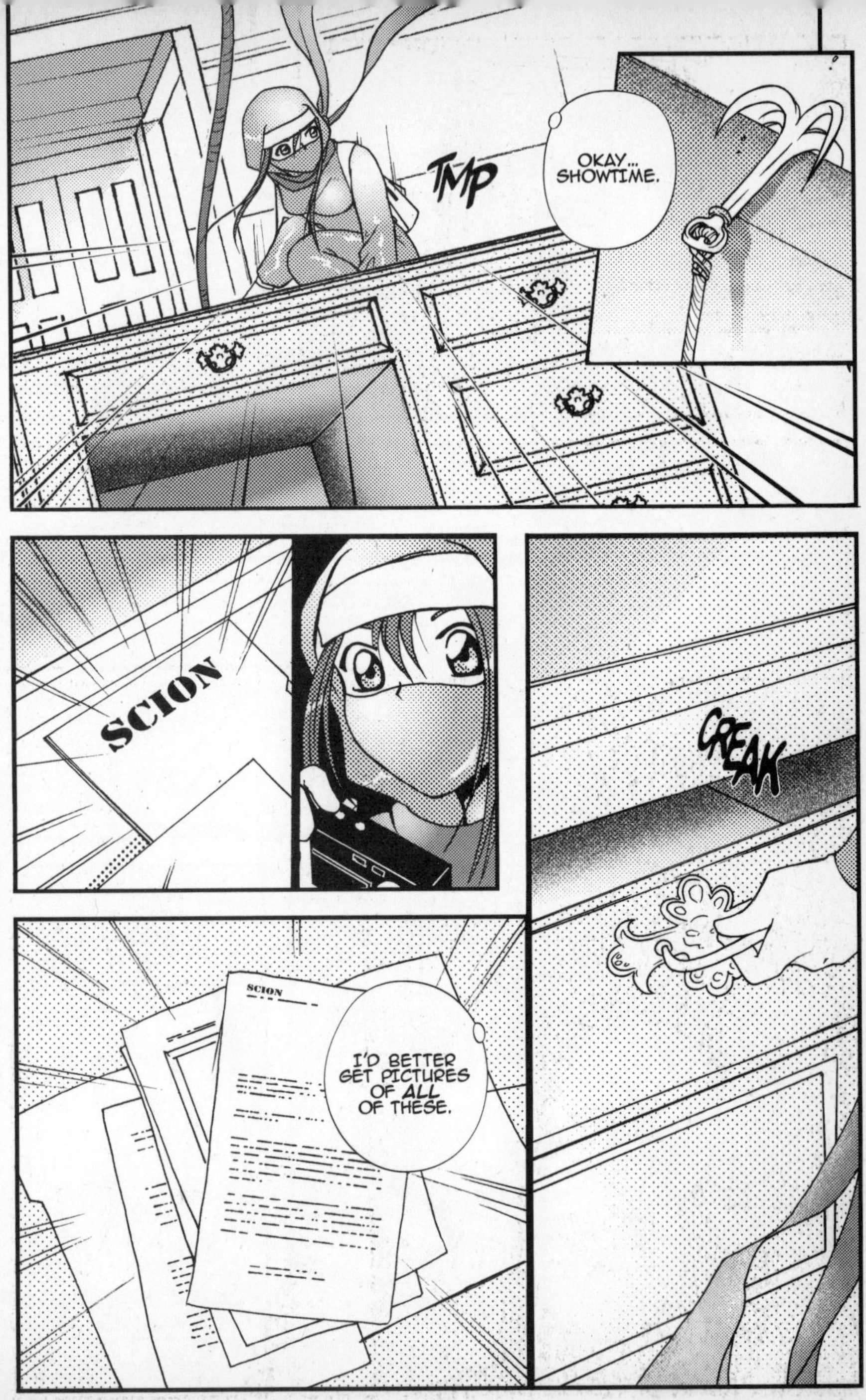

TMP

OKAY... SHOWTIME.

SCION

CREAK

SCION

I'D BETTER GET PICTURES OF *ALL* OF THESE.

PIECE OF CAKE.
CLICK CLICK CLICK CLICK
YAY, ME!
UH-OH.
CREAK
I SEE I HAVE AN *UNWELCOME* GUEST.
HOW *DARE* YOU BREAK INTO *MY* EMBASSY?!

I KNOW WHAT YOU'RE THINKING. 'HIS COUNTRY IS SMALL. I CAN DO WHATEVER I WANT.'
BUT APPEARANCES CAN BE DECEIVING, MY STEALTHY FRIEND...
SHNK
...AND SIZE ISN'T EVERYTHING!

SLICE
THUMP!
IT'S *RUDE* TO LEAVE WITHOUT SAYING GOODBYE TO YOUR HOST.
DON'T THEY TEACH YOU *ANYTHING* IN NINJA SCHOOL OR SPY SCHOOL OR WHEREVER THEY TRAIN YOU TO BREAK INTO EMBASSIES?

ER... THAT IS, AS SOON AS I GET MY SWORD OUT OF MY GRAND-FATHER'S HEAD.
NOW, I WILL GIVE YOU A LESSON IN MANNERS.
SPRANG!
SWIPE!
RUNNING AWAY AGAIN?

TMP
GULP!
STOMP
STOMP
STOMP
STOMP
PERHAPS I WAS A BIT HASTY...
GUARDS!
...

THIS GUY
NEVER
SHUTS UP.
EEK!
SPRING
BONG!
BONK

TMP

GULP!

STOMP
STOMP
STOMP
STOMP

PERHAPS I WAS A BIT HASTY...

...

GUARDS!

YES SIR!
NOW THEY WILL GIVE YOU A LESSON IN MANNERS.
YES SIR!
YES SIR!
O COUNT, MY COUNT!
CHAAARGE!
GET HER!
WOW. THIS IS A LOT OF GUYS.
SHOULD BE FUN!

IT'S ONE GIRL! DO SOMETHING YOU MORONS!

THIS GUY
NEVER
SHUTS UP.
SPRING
EEK!
BONK
BONG!

SNATCH

TIME TO GO.

SHOOT HER! SHE'S GOT MY--

--SWORD.

THUNK!

THAT WAS FUN AND A PERFECT MISSION SUCCESS!
CONTROL IS GONNA BE SO--
CRASH!
OUCH!

EXCUSE ME, MISS... THAT WAS ENTIRELY MY FAULT.
OH... WOW... IT'S THE BOY FROM BEFORE...

LET ME HELP YOU UP.
I'M SORRY. WHAT?
LET ME HELP YOU UP.
NO, I'M...
OH, OKAY... YOU CAN HELP ME UP.
I DIDN'T NOTICE HOW CUTE HE WAS BEFORE.
YOU SPEAK ENGLISH. ARE YOU FROM AMERICA OR BRUCKENSTEIN?

FIND HER!
I'M--
I'M SORRY. I HAVE TO GO.
I HOPE WE MEET AGAIN.
EXCUSE ME, SIR...
DID YOU SEE--
--A MOST FASCINATING GIRL?

YES.
YES, I DID.

AGENT LUNA, THIS MISSION WAS A COMPLETE AND UTTER **FAILURE**.

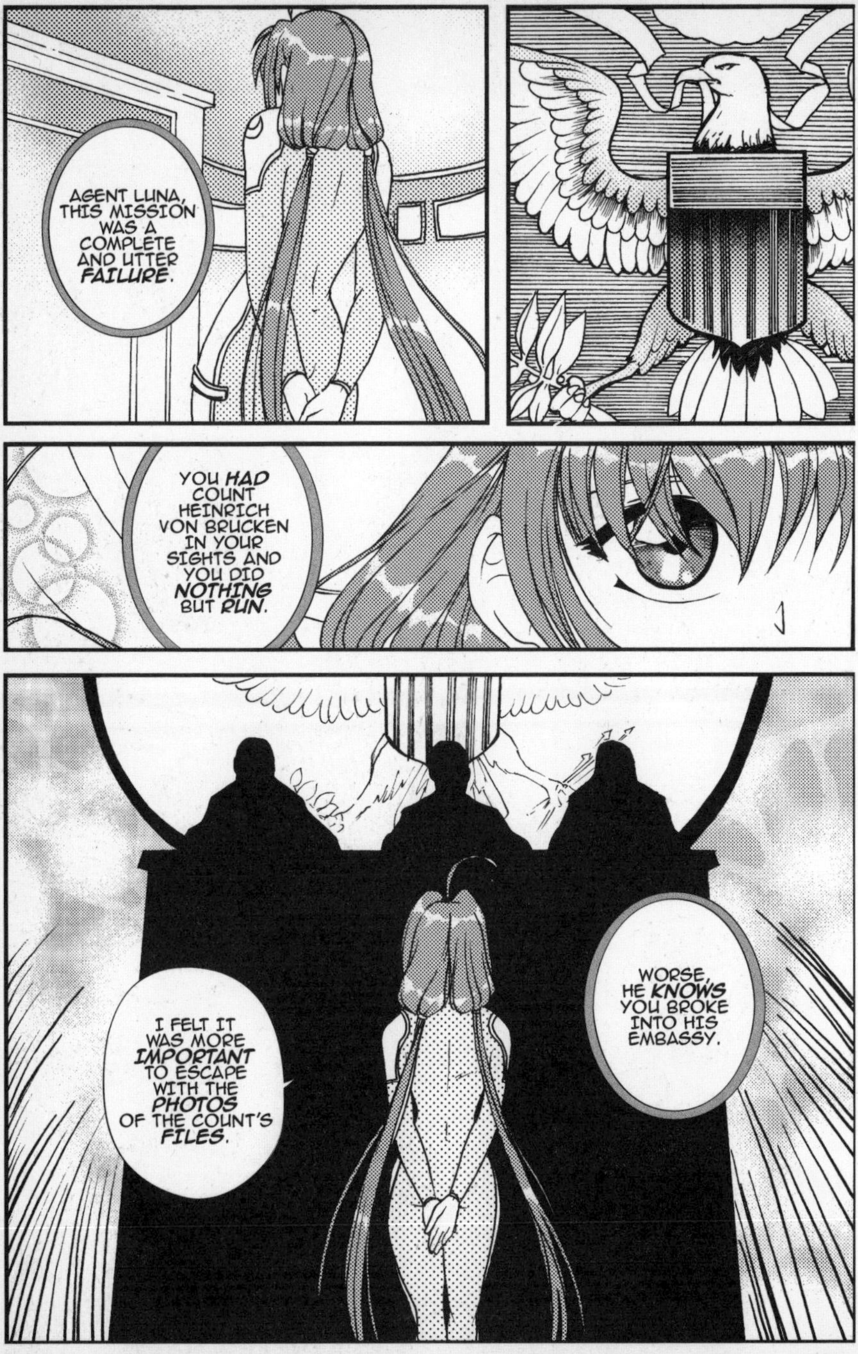

YOU **HAD** COUNT HEINRICH VON BRUCKEN IN YOUR SIGHTS AND YOU DID **NOTHING** BUT **RUN**.

WORSE, HE **KNOWS** YOU BROKE INTO HIS EMBASSY.
I FELT IT WAS MORE **IMPORTANT** TO ESCAPE WITH THE **PHOTOS** OF THE COUNT'S **FILES**.

CONTROL, REPORT!
LET'S SEE WHAT YOUR CONTROL AGENT HAS TO SAY ABOUT YOUR FAILURE.
YOU SHOULD HAVE FINISHED HIM WHEN YOU HAD THE CHANCE. THEN THE FILES WOULD BE IRRELEVANT.
BUT HAD SHE STAYED TO BATTLE VON BRUCKEN--
WITH ALL DUE RESPECT, SIR, THAT WAS NOT HER MISSION. MOREOVER, BRUCKENSTEIN MAY BE A ROGUE NATION, BUT IT IS A MEMBER OF THE UNITED NATIONS. ATTACKING ITS LEADER WOULD SUBJECT THE U.S. AND THIS AGENCY TO SCRUTINY.
DIRECTORS, I BELIEVE YOUR CRITICISM OF AGENT LUNA IS ONE HUNDRED PERCENT UNFOUNDED.
MY AGENT'S MISSION WAS TO FIND OUT ABOUT THE COUNT'S LATEST OPERATION.
SHE GOT ACCESS TO HIS FILES AND PHOTOS OF ONE OF HIS CONTACTS. THAT IS MISSION SUCCESS.
YOUR ASSESSMENT IS VALID. WE WILL DISCUSS HOW TO PROCEED.
YOU ARE BOTH DISMISSED.

BUT-
THAT WAS A MAJOR SCREW-UP, AND I DON'T LIKE IT WHEN MY AGENTS SCREW UP.
THEY WERE RIGHT. YOU HAD A SHOT AT ENDING THIS WHOLE THING BEFORE THE COUNT LAUNCHES HIS SCHEME.
CONTROL, THANKS FOR BACKING ME UP IN THERE. I THOUGHT THEY WERE BEING A LITTLE HARSH.
BUT YOU STOOD UP FOR ME IN THERE. WHAT YOU SAID TO THE DIRECTORS...?
WAAA!
DON'T YOU EVER MAKE ME DEFEND YOUR FAILURES AGAIN.
A LOT OF TIME, ENERGY AND MONEY WAS INVESTED IN YOU, LUNA. FROM THE TEST TUBE, TO YOUR SCHOOLING, TO YOUR TRAINING.
MY AGENT WAS BEING MADE TO LOOK BAD. AND THAT MAKES ME LOOK BAD.

YES. BECAUSE I 'KID' OFTEN.
Dr. ANDY COLLINS, Phd

YOU'RE KIDDING ME?

SHE WAS REALLY *CRYING*?

MAYBE IT'S THE *ISOLATION* IN WHICH YOU RAISED HER. OR MAYBE IT'S THE *GENETIC* ENGINEERING.

MAYBE THAT'S THE *PROBLEM*. HER MOODS ARE LIKE ANY OTHER TEENAGER'S, BUT MORE *EXTREME*.

NATURAL FOR A FIFTEEN YEAR OLD, SURE. *NOT* NATURAL FOR A SPECIALLY BRED, SPECIALLY TRAINED *SECRET AGENT*.

WE KNEW THIS WOULD COME. SHE'S GOING TO GO THROUGH SOME *ROUGH* EMOTIONAL TIMES.

EITHER WAY, IT'S A *PROBLEM*. I NEED HER IN THE FIELD *NOW*.

KNOWN TO THE REST OF THE WORLD AS *ADOLESCENCE*.

AND I MUST SAY, MY ADOLESCENCE WAS NOT NEARLY SO ROUGH.

YOU WERE BROUGHT HERE, DR. COLLINS, TO ***HANDLE*** THOSE 'ROUGH' TIMES.

SLAM

YOU AND ME? IN THE FIELD? TOGETHER?

YOU'RE KIDDING?

AS I SAID, I NEVER KID.

TOMORROW. BE READY. WE'RE SENDING HER IN.

WE'RE SENDING YOU **IN** BECAUSE **EVERY** FILE YOU BROUGHT US WAS OF SOMEONE IN **THERE**.

WE DON'T THINK THEY **ALL** WORK FOR VON BRUCKEN.

HEY, MAYBE NONE OF THEM DO. THEY MAY JUST BE **NICE** AND **NORMAL**.

GET TO **KNOW** THEM. FIND OUT IF THEY WORK FOR THE COUNT. OR, IF NOT, WHY HE'S INTERESTED IN THEM.
DON'T WORRY. YOU'RE GOOD AT THIS. YOU'LL DO **FINE**. THEY'LL ALL **LIKE** YOU.

NOW LET'S GO.
GOSSIP
GIGGLE
CHATTER
TALK
BRAG
CHATTER
GET IN THERE AND DON'T LET ME DOWN.
HAVE A GOOD FIRST DAY AT SCHOOL. I KNOW YOU CAN HANDLE IT.

File 02
NOBEL HIGH

WHO'S THE NEW GIRL?
NO IDEA.
CHECK OUT THE FRESH MEAT.
I LIKE IT MUCH BETTER WHEN WE KNOW ABOUT THE NEW STUDENTS BEFORE THEY GET HERE.
I MEAN, DOES ANYBODY KNOW ANYTHING ABOUT THIS GIRL?

'SCUSE ME.
HEADS UP!
COMING
THROUGH!
WHOA...
...WHO'S
SHE?

DORK?

HELLO?

WATCH WHERE YOU'RE GOING!

RAZZIN-
FRAZZIN-
PLASTIC--

HEY, THERE... SORRY ABOUT ELIZABETH.
SHE'S HAVING A BAD DAY.

WHEN DOES SHE EVER HAVE GOOD DAYS?
HER BIRTHDAY. WHEN THE NEW FALL FASHIONS COME OUT.

FRANCESCA! WE'RE WALKING HERE.
SLUM ON YOUR OWN TIME. OLIVER RIGGS IS NOT WORTHY OF MINE.

GOTTA GO. SEE YOU LATER.

YEAH. 'SEE YOU LATER.' NOT LIKELY.

HEY! WHERE'D THE NEW GIRL GO?

THANK YOU BOTH FOR COMING.

I FIND THAT THE MORE ***INVOLVED*** THE PARENTS ARE, THE MORE ***FULFILLED*** THE CHILD IS.

PRINCIPAL

NOW... MR. AND MRS. COLLINS, WHY DON'T YOU TELL ME ABOUT YOUR DAUGHTER?

EXCUSE ME, PRINCIPAL OHLINGER, BUT I GO BY MS. KAJIWARA.

OH, I AM ***SO*** SORRY.

I USED TO LISTEN TO YOUR RADIO SHOW ALL THE TIME. WHY DID IT GO OFF THE AIR?
I WENT INTO *PRIVATE* PRACTICE.

I SEE... THAT'S A REAL SHAME.
NOW, IS THERE ANYTHING WE SHOULD KNOW ABOUT LUNA?

WE JUST LIKE TO KNOW OF ANY HOME SITUATIONS SO WE CAN TAILOR THE LEARNING EXPERIENCE FOR EACH CHILD.
A VERY *WISE* WAY OF TEACHING.
THANK YOU, DR. COLLINS. FROM YOU, THAT'S *HIGH* PRAISE.

WE JUST WANT TO MAKE SURE THAT THE... *INTERPERSONAL* SITUATIONS... DO NOT GET IN THE WAY OF HER STUDIES.

JENNIFER AND I HAVE... HOME-SCHOOLED LUNA UP TIL NOW.
SHE'S NEW TO THE SOCIAL NUANCES OF HIGH SCHOOL.

LET ME EXPLAIN HOW NOBEL HIGH WORKS. THIS IS THE FINEST HIGH SCHOOL IN THE COUNTRY.
AND TO US, EVERY CHILD HAS A STORY ALL THEIR OWN.

THE STUDENTS HERE ARE THE CHILDREN OF DIPLOMATS, SCIENTISTS AND LEADERS FROM ALL AROUND THE WORLD.
YOU NEEDN'T SELL US ON THE SCHOOL. OUR DAUGHTER IS ALREADY HERE.

FITTING IN IS DIFFICULT FOR **ALL** OF THEM. LUNA'S SITUATION ISN'T ANY ***DIFFERENT***.

CLASS, WE HAVE A NEW STUDENT TODAY.

I THINK WE'LL HAVE LUNA UP TO SPEED, SOCIALLY SPEAKING, IN NO TIME.

THIS IS LUNA COLLINS.
SHE JUST TRANSFERRED TO NOBEL HIGH AND WE SHOULD ALL MAKE HER FEEL WELCOME.
LUNA, WHY DON'T YOU TELL US SOMETHING ABOUT YOURSELF?

ELIZABETH WESTBROOK, THAT IS NOT HOW WE MAKE PEOPLE FEEL WELCOME.

YEAH, LIKE WHERE DID YOU GET THOSE SHOES?
I MEAN, FOR SOMETHING TO BE RETRO IT NEEDS TO BE AT LEAST TEN YEARS OLD, NOT LAST SEASON'S STYLE.

IS SOMETHING WRONG WITH MY SHOES?

YOU'RE FINE, LUNA.

HA HA HA HA HA HA HA HA
I CAN GO HOME AND CHANGE THEM.

FIND YOURSELF AN EMPTY SEAT AND WE'LL GET CLASS STARTED.

NO NEED TO CHANGE.

AND THIS IS AN EXPENSIVE BAG. IT NEEDS ITS OWN CHAIR.

SORRY. SHE DID SAY EMPTY.

YOU CAN SIT OVER HERE.
PSST... LUNA...

BEFORE YOU GO, I'D LIKE YOU TO MEET ARISTOTLE, THE SCHOOL MASCOT.
OH DEAR... HE'S ASLEEP.

EVEN THOUGH I HAVE BAD SHOES?

I'M SURE YOU DO.

BUT, OTHER THAN THAT, I THINK THIS HAS BEEN REMARKABLY *PRODUCTIVE*. I'M GLAD YOU CAME IN.
I LIKE TO THINK THAT AT NOBEL HIGH, WHEN A CHILD ENROLLS, THE WHOLE FAMILY ENROLLS.

IF I MAY... I SENSE A LITTLE... TENSION BETWEEN YOU AND YOUR HUSBAND.
IS EVERYTHING *OKAY* AT HOME BECAUSE —
PRINCIPAL OHLINGER, I'M SURE THERE ARE MANY WHO APPRECIATE YOUR HANDS-ON, NEW AGE APPROACH TO EDUCATION.
I, HOWEVER, WOULD PREFER YOU STICK TO THE STUDENTS AND LEAVE MY HOME LIFE OUT OF IT.

JENNIFER, DEAR... WE'VE TAKEN UP ENOUGH OF PRINCIPAL OHLINGER'S TIME. WE SHOULD *GO*.

YOU'RE ENJOYING THIS, AREN'T YOU?
A LITTLE.

PLEASE FORGIVE ME IF I'VE OVERSTEPPED ANY BOUNDS.
NOT AT ALL. NICE TO MEET YOU.
AND DON'T WORRY ABOUT US. THERE'S PLENTY OF *LOVE* IN OUR MARRIAGE.

LISTEN UP!
YOU WILL DO FIVE LAPS AROUND THE GYM IN TEN MINUTES.
AND I WANT TO SEE SOME HUSTLE OUT THERE!

WHEET!
NOW GO!
I HEAR HER FATHER IS SOME KIND OF DR. PHIL WANNABE. I MEAN, PLEASE...
AND HAVE YOU SEEN HER HAIR?
LOOK AT HER. WHAT A SHOW-OFF. WHO DOES SHE THINK SHE IS? MARION JONES?

WHY AREN'T YOU RUNNING, COLLINS?
I'M DONE, MR. DREYFUS. FIVE LAPS.
I SAID FIVE LAPS IN TEN MINUTES.
IT DOESN'T *TAKE* ME TEN MINUTES. THIS WAS *EASY*.
I WON'T BE HAVING ANYONE *SLACKING* OFF IN MY CLASS. GIVE ME FIVE *MORE* LAPS!
BUT—
KIDS...

I HEAR HER MOM WORKS FOR THE GOVERNMENT BUT NO ONE KNOWS WHAT SHE DOES.
MAYBE HER MOM'S A SECRETARY IN THE DEPARTMENT OF POINTLESS BUREAUCRACY.
MAYBE HER MOTHER'S A *SPY*.
'SCUSE ME!
CRASH

CLUNK
OW! HEY, I SAID I WAS SORRY.
SORRY ABOUT YOUR LUNCH.
FOOD SUCKS HERE ANYWAY.
WHOA...
THERE SHE IS AGAIN.
OKAY, OLIVER... TIME TO MAKE YOUR MOVE. SHE'S TOO NEW TO THE SCHOOL TO REALIZE THAT NO ONE LIKES YOU.

HEY THERE.

SO... YOU'RE THE ***NEW*** GIRL, RIGHT?

YES! I'M THE NEW GIRL!

AND MY SHOES ARE OUT OF FASHION AND I THINK I'M SOME GIRL NAMED MARION JONES, WHATEVER THAT MEANS! AND MY MOM'S A SECRETARY!

I MEAN, IF YOUR MOM IS A SECRETARY, THAT'S COOL.

ANYTHING ELSE YOU WANT TO ADD?

HEY, IT'S OKAY.

MY DAD IS A SECURITY GUARD AT THE U.N. AND THAT'S THE ONLY REASON I'M HERE AT THIS SCHOOL.

OH, I'M SORRY. I THOUGHT YOU CAME TO MAKE FUN OF THE NEW GIRL.
NO, 'COURSE NOT.

YOU WERE EATING ALONE AND I—
MR. RIGGS!

HOW MANY TIMES HAVE I TOLD YOU *NOT* TO SKATEBOARD IN THE SCHOOL?

YOU'RE IN *BIG* TROUBLE, BUSTER.

AND CROWDED WITH PEOPLE!

BUT THAT WAS IN THE HALLWAYS WHICH WERE CROWDED WITH PEOPLE. THIS IS THE LUNCHROOM. IT'S WIDE OPEN AND--

LET'S GO.
MARION JONES IS AN OLYMPIC RUNNER, BY THE WAY.
SO AT LEAST THEY THOUGHT YOU WERE *FAST*.
HEY, THE NEW GIRL JUST GOT OLIVER IN TROUBLE.
SLAM

TALK
CHATTER
LAUGH
GOSSIP
LAUGH

I WONDER HOW SHE DID.

HI, LUNA.
HOW WAS YOUR DAY, LUNA?
WELL? REPORT.
COME ON, GET IN. WE HAVE SOMETHING TO SHOW YOU.
TERRIBLE.

HERE WE ARE.
THIS IS OUR NEW HOUSE.
WHAT DO YOU THINK?
I DON'T LIKE IT. CAN'T WE GO BACK TO THE BASE?

LUNA! WHAT ABOUT YOUR REPORT?

I SAID I DON'T LIKE IT.

BUT YOU'VE GOT A BEAUTIFUL BEDROOM ON THE SECOND FLOOR. LOTS OF SPACE...

NO ONE WOULD **TALK** TO ME. THEY ALL **HATE** ME. EXCEPT ONE BOY. HE WAS NICE. BUT THEN MR. DREYFUS TOOK HIM AWAY!

I DON'T **HAVE** A REPORT.

I TOLD YOU SHE WASN'T READY—
DON'T SAY A WORD.
SLAM

MAYBE MR. DREYFUS WORKS FOR COUNT VON BRUCKEN! HE'S CERTAINLY **MEAN** ENOUGH.

WHOOSH
CLUNK
HEY!
ARE YOU OKAY?
OW!
ME? I'M COOL. TOTALLY DID THAT ON PURPOSE.
I'M OLIVER, BY THE WAY. WE... UM... DIDN'T GET TO THAT PART YESTERDAY.
I'M LUNA.
YEAH, I KNOW.

HI.

I'M FRANCESCA. YOU'RE IN MY SCIENCE CLASS.

AREN'T YOU FRIENDS WITH THAT GIRL WHO HATES ME?

ELIZABETH DOESN'T HATE YOU. SHE'S JUST... TOUGH ON NEW KIDS. SHE RULES THIS SCHOOL AND YOU MIGHT THREATEN--

RULES? HOW? LIKE A DICTATOR?
YEAH. KINDA LIKE A DICTATOR.

HOW DOES SHE ENFORCE IT? DOES SHE HAVE SOLDIERS?
SOLDIERS? NO SOLDIERS. SHE ENFORCES IT BY MAKING EVERYONE ELSE MISERABLE.
NO... SHE'S JUST SOCIALLY ON TOP AND HAS TO WORRY ABOUT EVERY NEW STUDENT THREATENING THAT.

HEY, CHECK OUT THE NEW KID!

I AM SO TIRED OF EVERYONE TALKING ABOUT--

...ME.

WELL CONGRATULATIONS. YOU'RE NOT THE NEW KID ANYMORE.

THE BOY FROM PARIS!

OH, I HEARD ABOUT HIM. WE'VE BEEN WAITING FOR THIS ONE. HE'S GOING TO MAKE THINGS ***VERY*** INTERESTING AROUND HERE.

IT'S SUCH A SCANDAL.

WHY? WHO IS HE?

THAT'S JONAH VON BRUCKEN. FROM BRUCKENSTEIN. HIS FATHER IS ...
...COUNT HEINRICH VON BRUCKEN.

IN YOUR DREAMS

WRITING PROCESS

File 03
BAD BOY

HEY, MAN... YOU NEED SOMEONE TO SHOW YOU AROUND?

ARE YOU IN MISS HOLLINGSWORTH'S HOMEROOM? BECAUSE IF YOU WANT, I COULD--

YOU LIKE FOOTBALL? WE COULD GET YOU ON THE TEAM.

DO I LOOK LIKE I PLAY FOOTBALL?

THE MORE HE IGNORES THEM, THE MORE THEY WANT TO BE AROUND HIM.
LOOK AT HIM.
IT'S GENIUS!
GENIUS?
THIS IS GOING TO BE FUN.
WATCH AND LEARN, GIRLS.

THUD
HEY! WATCH WHERE YOU'RE GOING!
HMPH. SOME PEOPLE.
WHAT DID YOU DO THAT FOR? I THOUGHT YOU *WANTED* TO TALK TO HIM.
THE ONLY WAY TO GET THROUGH TO A BOY LIKE THAT IS PRETEND YOU DON'T CARE.

YOU HAVE TO WORK IT. IT'S NOT LIKE HE'D JUST WALK UP TO ANY OLD GIRL AND SAY HI.

UM... ELIZABETH...

I BET HE'S WONDERING ABOUT ME RIGHT NOW.

HER?!
EXCUSE ME?
OH NO! IF HE RECOGNIZES ME FROM PARIS, I'M IN BIG TROUBLE.
EEP
LUNA!

LUNA? IS THAT YOUR NAME?
NO! UH... YES.
I'M PRETTY SURE WE HAVE. IN PARIS?
HAVE WE MET BEFORE? YOU LOOK FAMILIAR.
UM, NO, I DON'T THINK SO.
I'VE NEVER BEEN TO PARIS. NEVER.
I'D REMEMBER SOMEONE LIKE YOU. ARE YOU SURE?
I'VE NEVER BEEN TO PARIS!!!
SHE HAD A DOUBLE MOCHACHINO THIS MORNING. CAFFEINE... YOU KNOW...

SO, UH... WELL, JUST REMEMBER THAT.
YEAH, WELL, YOU MAY BE WAY COOLER THAN ME, BUT I SAW LUNA FIRST.
SO, NEW GUY, HUH?
I JUST... I HAVE NEVER BEEN TO PARIS. HE CLEARLY THINKS I'M SOMEONE ELSE.
PANT PANT
WHY DID YOU LEAVE? THE CUTEST GUY EVER COMES TO NOBEL HIGH, SEEKS YOU OUT AND YOU WALK AWAY?
WHAT BOOK?
LUNA! THAT'S THE OLDEST TRICK IN THE BOOK.

IT GIVES YOU A REASON TO TALK TO SOMEONE.
HOW TO PICK UP GIRLS 101. "HAVE WE MET?" IT'S JUST A LINE.
REALLY? SO YOU DON'T THINK HE RECOGNIZED ME?
NO. IT WAS TOTALLY A LINE.
THAT'S A RELIEF.
RRRRRRING!
COME ON. WE'LL BE LATE FOR CLASS.
FRANCESCA? WHERE CAN I BUY THIS HOW TO BOOK?
...
UH... LUNA? IT'S NOT A REAL BOOK.

YES, MA'AM. I HAD NO IDEA HE WAS ATTENDING NOBEL HIGH.

DINNER!

WHAT ARE YOU DOING? WE'RE DEBRIEFING.

IT'S DINNER TIME, JENNIFER.

YOU WILL CALL ME CONTROL.
WE HAVE A COVER TO MAINTAIN. YOU ARE MY WIFE. LUNA IS MY DAUGHTER.
AND SOMEONE NEEDS TO MAKE SURE SHE EATS.
RELAX. WE CAN KILL TWO BIRDS WITH ONE STONE.
CONTINUE, LUNA. TELL US ABOUT YOUR DAY AT SCHOOL.
WOW. THIS IS REALLY GOOD.
LUNA, PLEASE CONTINUE YOUR REPORT.
SORRY. SO I WAS REALLY NERVOUS WHEN I SAW HIM.
NERVOUS? WHY?

OH... DID I FORGET TO MENTION THE PART WHERE I RAN INTO HIM BOTH BEFORE AND AFTER BREAKING INTO THE EMBASSY?

WELL... I WASN'T SURE IF HE'D RECOGNIZE ME FROM PARIS.
PARIS?

WHAT?! YOUR COVER COULD BE SERIOUSLY COMPROMISED!
JENNIFER... YOU'RE NOT HELPING HERE.

I DIDN'T *KNOW* HE WAS VON BRUCKEN'S SON. HE WAS JUST A BOY.

LUNA, WHY DIDN'T YOU TELL US ABOUT SEEING HIM BEFORE?

I'M SORRY. I JUST... IT DIDN'T SEEM *IMPORTANT* AT THE TIME.

HE THOUGHT I LOOKED FAMILIAR.
BUT I TOLD HIM I'D NEVER BEEN TO PARIS.
FAIR ENOUGH. NOW WHAT HAPPENED TODAY AT SCHOOL?
GOOD. THAT'S GOOD. AND DID HE BELIEVE YOU?
I THINK SO. THIS OTHER GIRL TOLD ME HE DIDN'T RECOGNIZE ME, THAT HE WAS ONLY TRYING TO TALK TO ME.
THEN WE'RE FINE.
SHE SAYS IT'S PART OF SOME DATING PLAYBOOK BOYS HAVE.
AH, YES... I REMEMBER THE PLAYBOOK.
YOU REALIZE THAT'S NOT A LITERAL BOOK, LUNA?
OF COURSE I DO.

ALRIGHT, WE HAVE A ***GOLDEN*** OPPORTUNITY HERE. YOU WILL KEEP A CLOSE EYE ON THIS BOY AND REPORT BACK ***EVERYTHING*** HE DOES.

YES, MA'AM. I WILL BEGIN SURVEILLANCE TOMORROW.

BUT BE CAREFUL IN CASE HE ***DOES*** KNOW WHO YOU ARE AND CAN PLACE YOU AT THE EMBASSY BREAK-IN.

RIGHT... I'LL LEAVE THE SPY WORK TO YOU LADIES.

MAYBE COUNT VON BRUCKEN HAD ALL THOSE FILES ON THE STUDENTS SIMPLY TO SEE WHAT SORT OF CLASSMATES HIS SON WOULD HAVE.

THERE HE IS.
HE'S MAKING NOTES. MAYBE FOR HIS FATHER'S PLAN.
I WILL HAVE TO ACQUIRE HIS NOTEBOOK LATER.

RRRING

THAT CLASS WAS *SO* BORING. RIGHT, JONAH?

ARE YOU GOING TO LUNCH, JONAH? WE COULD EAT TOGETHER?

YOU LOOK SMART, JONAH. MAYBE YOU COULD HELP ME WITH THE HOMEWORK?

NOT RIGHT NOW. I HAVE SOMETHING TO DO.

HE'S NOT GOING TO LUNCH LIKE EVERYONE ELSE. WHAT COULD HE BE UP TO?

HE'S LOOKING FOR SOMETHING.

LEAVE IT TO VON BRUCKEN TO USE HIS SON TO CARRY OUT HIS DIRTY DEEDS.

BUT I'LL REPORT THIS TO CONTROL.

SHE'LL BE PLEASED WITH MY WORK.

AND--
HEY. WE MEET AGAIN. MY NAME'S JONAH.
GULP

SHE'S SHIER THAN I THOUGHT.

YOU GOING TO THE GAME?

OF COURSE.

NOBEL OWLS VS BASKERVILL HOUNDS

THIS FRIDAY AT 7:30
NOBEL OWLS VS BAS RVILLE
THE OWLS ARE GONNA KICK SOME BASKERVILLE BUTT.
THIS FRIDAY
LOOKS LIKE THE NEW GUY'S AN OWLS FAN.
HELLO THERE... ARISTOTLE.

HUH?
HEY THERE.
. . . . .
OLIVER. WE MET YESTERDAY. OUT HERE IN FACT.
RIGHT. SO, UM, WHAT'RE YOU DOING?
HE-LLLO!

RIGHT. DUMB QUESTION. OKAY, ***WHY*** ARE YOU LOOKING AT THE OWL?

I THINK HE'S COOL.

LOOKING AT THE OWL.

YEAH, I'M JUST NOT SEEING IT. HE'S JUST... SLEEPING.

HE'S ***NOCTURNAL***. A CREATURE OF THE NIGHT. I LIKE THAT. BESIDES, HE'S ONLY HALF ASLEEP.

WATCH HIM, YOU'LL SEE. HE ***KNOWS*** WE'RE HERE.

OKAY...

I THINK I'LL LEAVE YOU TWO ***ALONE***.

YOU'RE FRIENDS WITH LUNA.
YEAH, ME AND HER, WE GO WAY BACK.
TELL ME ABOUT HER.
WEREN'T YOU LISTENING YESTERDAY WHEN I TOLD YOU I SAW HER FIRST?
DUDE, I AM *SO* NOT GIVING YOU THE SCOOP ON HER.
NOT REALLY, NO.

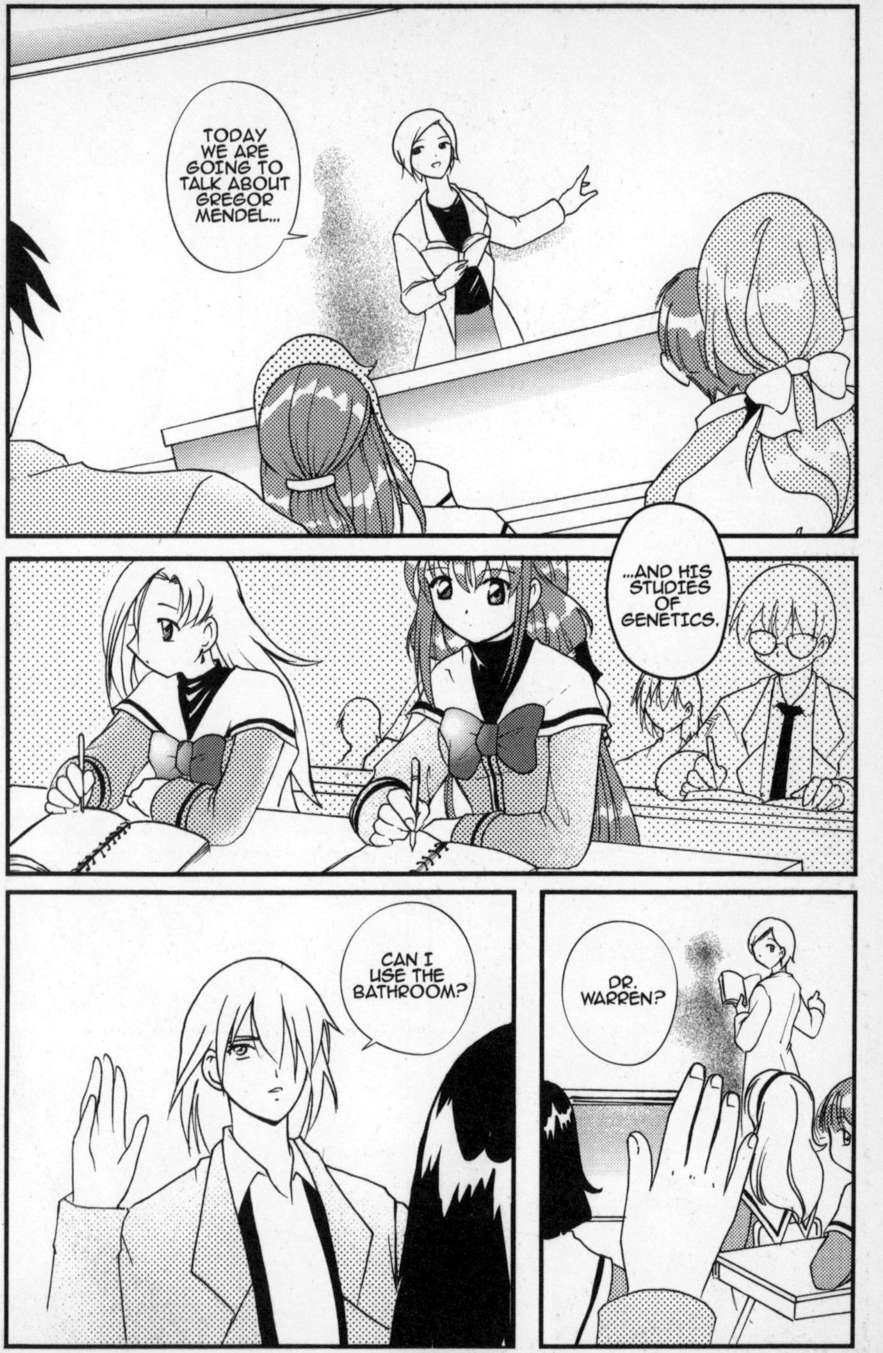

TODAY WE ARE GOING TO TALK ABOUT GREGOR MENDEL...

...AND HIS STUDIES OF GENETICS.

GO AHEAD, JONAH. JUST HURRY BACK.
HE *SO* LIKES YOU.
DO YOU THINK SO?

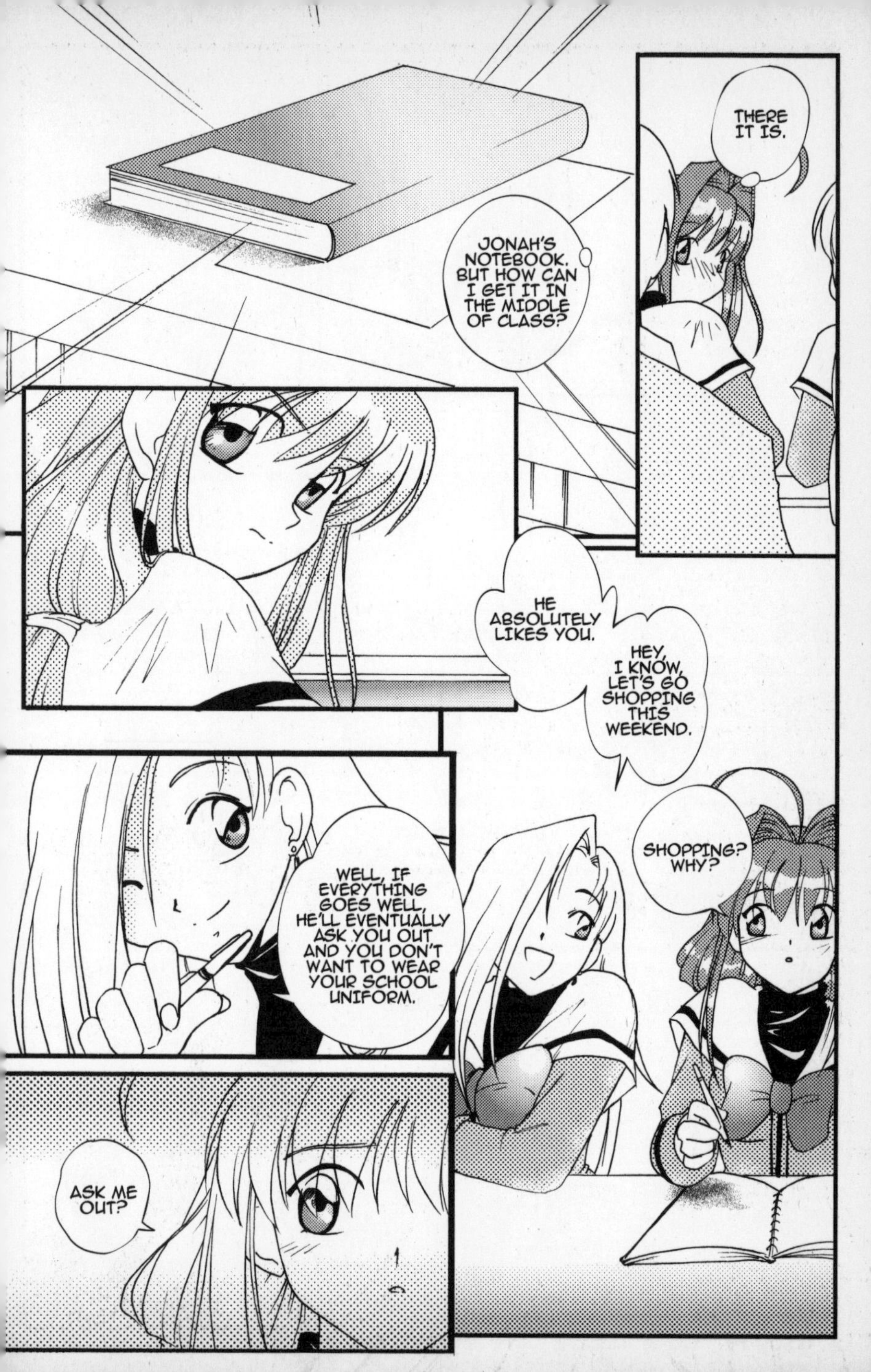
THERE IT IS.
JONAH'S NOTEBOOK. BUT HOW CAN I GET IT IN THE MIDDLE OF CLASS?
HE ABSOLUTELY LIKES YOU.
HEY, I KNOW, LET'S GO SHOPPING THIS WEEKEND.
SHOPPING? WHY?
WELL, IF EVERYTHING GOES WELL, HE'LL EVENTUALLY ASK YOU OUT AND YOU DON'T WANT TO WEAR YOUR SCHOOL UNIFORM.
ASK ME OUT?

DEFINITELY. A GUY LIKE HIM WON'T WAIT LONG TO MAKE HIS MOVE.
DOCTOR WARREN!
ARISTOTLE'S GONE!
SOMEONE TOOK HIM!

I'M TELLING YOU, IT WAS THAT NEW GUY.

JONAH WOULDN'T DO THIS.

OH YEAH! I SAW HIM STARING AT ARISTOTLE TODAY LIKE HE WAS HIS GIRLFRIEND OR SOMETHING.

THAT GUY'S NOT RIGHT IN THE HEAD.

HELLO, I'M HOME!
HEY, LUNA. HOW WAS SCHOOL?
GOOD. IT WAS ACTUALLY GOOD.
FRANCESCA INVITED ME TO GO SHOPPING THIS WEEKEND. SHE THINKS JONAH MIGHT ASK ME OUT.
AND THAT'S GOOD, RIGHT? BECAUSE THEN I CAN REALLY KEEP AN EYE ON HIM--

OWL? WHAT'S GOING ON?
ARE YOU GOING TO TELL US ABOUT THE OWL?
OH YEAH. SOMEONE TOOK ARISTOTLE. BUT FRANCESCA THINKS HE'LL TURN UP TOMORROW.
AND?
AND WHAT?
YOU'RE KIDDING, RIGHT? YOU THINK A MISSING MASCOT FALLS UNDER THE AGENCY'S BUSINESS?
DOES SHE? AND WHERE DID FRANCESCA STUDY INVESTIGATIVE SKILLS? LUNA, YOU'RE NOT FOCUSING.
I THINK THAT THE SON OF ONE OF THE MOST *DANGEROUS* MEN OUT THERE ARRIVES AT THIS SCHOOL AND THE VERY NEXT DAY SOMETHING WEIRD HAPPENS.
I THINK MY AGENT HAS FORGOTTEN *EVERYTHING* SHE'S LEARNED.
NO, CONTROL. I'LL BE BETTER. I ALMOST HAD A CHANCE TO STEAL JONAH'S NOTEBOOK TODAY.

NO, LUNA. YOUR PERFORMANCE IS COMPLETELY UNACCEPTABLE. THIS WAS A MISTAKE.

WE'RE PULLING YOU OUT OF NOBEL HIGH.

File 04
FIRST CRUSH

YOU'RE BEING IRRATIONAL.
I AM NEVER IRRATIONAL.
FORGIVE ME. YOU'RE BEING STUPID.

SHE'S A TEENAGER AND WE'VE JUST DROPPED HER INTO HIGH SCHOOL. OF COURSE SHE'S WORRIED ABOUT FRIENDS AND BOYS.
RIIING
YOU'RE RIGHT. IT IS NATURAL. WHICH IS WHY HER BEING THERE IS A *MISTAKE*.
AND THAT WAS MY CONCERN TOO, IF YOU REMEMBER. BUT MAYBE THIS IS THE BEST THING THAT COULD HAVE HAPPENED TO HER.
RIIING!
HELLO?

LUNA?
HI, WHAT'S GOING ON?
UH... YEAH.
COOL. GOT THE RIGHT NUMBER THEN. THIS IS FRANCESCA. FROM SCHOOL.

CLICK

I GOTTA GO, FRANCESCA.
THAT'S COOL. SEE YOU AT SCHOOL TOMORROW.
I HOPE SO.

IT HAS BEEN MADE CLEAR TO ME THAT IN THE INTEREST OF YOUR FUTURE TRAINING AS AN AGENT...
...WE SHOULD PERHAPS LET YOU COME TO TERMS WITH YOUR ADOLESCENCE.
AND THAT HIGH SCHOOL IS THE BEST PLACE FOR THAT.
I GET TO HAVE FRIENDS?

WHILE THERE IS GREAT RISK IN JONAH VON BRUCKEN FIGURING OUT WHO YOU ARE, THERE IS ALSO A LOT TO BE GAINED FROM GETTING CLOSE TO HIM.
ARE YOU KIDDING?

YOU NEED TO HAVE FRIENDS, LUNA. EVERYONE DOES.
FRIENDS ARE A VITAL SOURCE OF INTEL. HAVING A NETWORK IN PLACE CAN BE THE DIFFERENCE BETWEEN SUCCESS AND FAILURE.
YEAH, THAT'S WHY IT'S IMPORTANT.

I'LL DO IT, DR. ANDY. I CAN GET CLOSE TO HIM.
YOU SAID WE SHOULD ENCOURAGE HER TO EXPLORE HER FEELINGS.
WHICH IS NOT THE SAME AS TELLING HER TO GET INFO FROM THIS BOY.
LUNA, IF YOU HAVE A CRUSH ON JONAH, IT COULD BECOME... COMPLICATED.
NOT AT ALL. I'M A PROFESSIONAL. CONTROL TRAINED ME WELL.
GOOD. JUST REMEMBER YOUR PRIORITIES.

ELIZABETH! CHECK *THAT* OUT.

SOMETHING NEEDS TO BE *DONE* ABOUT THAT.
YEAH...

I'VE DECIDED.
GREAT! WHAT DID YOU DECIDE?
I'M GOING TO TALK TO JONAH.
WOW, THAT REALLY IS GREAT. GOOD FOR YOU!
GOOD FOR LUNA WHAT?

OH, YEAH... THE WORD IS BAD. HE'S BAD NEWS. BAD BAD. BAD.

THAT'S NOT GOOD. THAT'S THE OPPOSITE OF GOOD. WHAT'S THE WORD I'M LOOKING FOR?

LUNA'S GOING TO TALK TO JONAH.
HI, OLIVER!

SOUNDS GOOD TO ME.
NO! HE'S OWL-OBSESSED AND THERE'S A MISSING OWL.
HELLO?? THE GUY'S PROBABLY A CRIMINAL. REALLY DANGEROUS.

HE'S JONAH VON BRUCKEN. AS IN BRUCKENSTEIN. AS IN, ROGUE NATION. HE'S ALL BROODY AND MYSTERIOUS AND DANGEROUS.
WHY?

NO, I'M GOOD. WHERE WAS I...?
TALKING ABOUT A CRIMINAL, I THINK.

OLIVER! LOOK OUT!
THUM
?!
OLIVER FAWL DOWN, GO BOOM...

HE SOUNDS LIKE BAD NEWS. TELL ME WHO HE IS AND I'LL AVOID HIM.

YEAH, WELL... I'D JUST AVOID MIRRORS IF I WERE YOU.

I'D BETTER MAKE SURE OLIVER DIDN'T... HURT HIMSELF.
YOU TWO... TALK.
FRANCESCA... WAIT.
WE JUST KEEP RUNNING INTO EACH OTHER.
I WASN'T IN PARIS!
WHO SAID ANYTHING ABOUT YOU FOLLOWING ME. I JUST SAID I SAW YOU IN THE LIBRARY. AND IT WAS... NICE.
I WASN'T FOLLOWING YOU. I LIKE BOOKS. I WANTED A BOOK.
YEAH... I GOT THAT. BUT YOU *WERE* IN THE LIBRARY YESTERDAY.

YEAH, NICE IS GOOD.

OH, NICE IS GOOD, RIGHT?

LUNA COLLINS! WHAT ARE YOU DOING HANGING AROUND A BOY LIKE JONAH VON BRUCKEN?

AND DO YOU KNOW WHAT TALKING LEADS TO?

WE'RE JUST TALKING.

...MORE TALKING?
BUT—
DON'T YOU GIVE ME SASS, BOY! DON'T YOU TWO HAVE CLASSES TO ATTEND?

DR. WARREN, THESE TWO SHOULD BE IN CLASS.
MR. DREYFUS...
...WILL YOU PLEASE STOP SCARING THE CHILDREN?
YOU TWO CONTINUE TALKING.
CLASSES HAVEN'T STARTED YET. THE CHILDREN CAN SOCIALIZE BEFORE THE BELL. WHY DON'T WE GET YOU A CUP OF COFFEE?
DECAF, PERHAPS?
BIRDS.
UH, DR. WARREN... WHAT'S THAT?

HEY, LOOK! IT'S ARISTOTLE!
THAT'S NOT ARISTOTLE. HE'S *HUGE!*
A LOT OF BIRDS.

SCREEECH!
THEY'VE GONE CRAZY! RUN FOR YOUR LIVES!
THEY ALL LOOK LIKE ARISTOTLE.
THEY'RE GONNA GET ME!

File 05
MYSTERIOUS BIRDS

I NEED TO DO SOMETHING. BUT IF ANYONE SEES ME... IF *JONAH* SEES ME...

GET DOWN!

EVERYONE INSIDE! INTO THE AUDITORIUM! NOW! NOW! NOW!
I GUESS THIS TIME, WE SHOULD LISTEN TO THAT JERK.
LUNA, LET'S GO.
LUNA...?

NO ONE SHOULD BE ABLE TO SEE ME OVER HERE.
I NEED TO GET TO HIGHER GROUND.
JUMP

TMP
HERE GOES NOTHING.
GREAT. GOT THEIR ATTENTION.
YOO-HOO! OWLIES! OVER HERE!
HEY THERE!

NOW WHAT?
THAT'S RIGHT. GOOD OWLS. FOLLOW ME.
I KNOW!
THE GYM!

I JUST NEED TO...
PERFECT!
COME ON OWLS!
EVERYONE INSIDE!

SCREECH!
SCREEECH!
AAAAAAAAAAH!

SCREE-URK!
A FEW MORE PASSES...
AND THAT'S...
...I DON'T ACTUALLY KNOW. TWO POINTS? WHAT DO YOU CALL IT?
I SHOULD ASK FRANCESCA ABOUT THE RULES OF VOLLEYBALL.

HMMMM...
SO THEY FOLLOWED ME INTO THE GYM. THEY HAVE A VOLLEYBALL NET THERE.
YOU NEVER TAUGHT ME HOW TO PLAY VOLLEYBALL, BY THE WAY.
A *REGRETTABLE* OVERSIGHT. FOCUS, LUNA.

AND WHO IS RESPONSIBLE FOR THE OWLS?

VERY WELL DONE, LUNA.
TASTE THIS.
SORRY. ANYWAY, I WRAPPED ALL THE OWLS UP INTO THE NET. AND NO ONE GOT HURT.

I DON'T KNOW YET, BUT I THINK I SHOULD INVESTIGATE MR. DREYFUS.
IS HE THE MOST LOGICAL SUSPECT?

WELL, HE DOESN'T LIKE KIDS A WHOLE LOT. AND WHO TEACHES HIGH SCHOOL IF THEY DON'T LIKE KIDS?

THAT'S VERY ASTUTE OF YOU, LUNA.

IT'S GOOD, BUT IT NEEDS MORE... I DON'T KNOW, SOMETHING.

FINE. YOU WILL INVESTIGATE THIS MR. DREYFUS.

I THINK I SHOULD GO BACK TONIGHT AND LOOK AROUND THE SCHOOL.
AGREED. MAKE SURE YOU WEAR YOUR STEALTH GEAR.
STEALTH GEAR? ARE YOU CRAZY?
I AM NOT CRAZY. IT'S STANDARD OPERATING PROCEDURE.
IT'S A SCHOOL AND SHE'S A *STUDENT*. IF SOMEONE SEES HER, SHE CAN VERY WELL SAY THAT SHE LEFT HER HOMEWORK IN HER LOCKER.
BUT IF SHE'S DRESSED LIKE A TEENAGE MUTANT NINJA--
I'LL WEAR NORMAL TEENAGE CLOTHES. IT'S OKAY, CONTROL. I CAN STILL BE STEALTHY.
FINE. GO. MY ORDERS CARRY NO WEIGHT AROUND HERE ANYWAY.

HUH? I THOUGHT WE WERE GOING TO STUDY. WONDER WHERE SHE'S GOING?
AND OLIVER RIGGS, WORLD-REKNOWNED X GAMES CHAMPION, PREPARES FOR THE FEAT OF A LIFETIME!
JUMP

MAN! HOW COME I'M ALWAYS FALLING WHEN I DO THIS DURING THE DAY?
TA-DA
BUT THE ONE TIME I DO IT PERFECTLY, THERE'S NO ONE--
--AROUND.
HEY, LUNA!
HEY, OLIVER...
I... I LEFT MY HOMEWORK IN MY LOCKER.
BUMMER. THEY LOCK THE SCHOOL UP PRETTY TIGHT AT NIGHT, BUT I KNOW A WAY IN.

HEY, LUNA!
I THOUGHT WE WERE GOING TO STUDY TONIGHT.
OH, COOL. I DIDN'T KNOW YOU BROUGHT FRANCESCA WITH YOU.
HI, FRANCESCA. I LEFT MY HOMEWORK IN MY LOCKER. OLIVER KNOWS A WAY INSIDE.
GREAT. HOW AM I SUPPOSED TO BE STEALTHY WITH THESE TWO AROUND?
CONTROL IS DEFINITELY GOING TO SAY 'I TOLD YOU SO' WHEN I GET HOME.
COOL! LET'S GO!

THIS IS A LOT OF WORK FOR HOMEWORK. YOU'RE REALLY SERIOUS ABOUT CATCHING UP QUICKLY.

SO WHAT HAPPENED TODAY WITH JONAH? AFTER ALL THAT FUSS WITH THE OWLS, I FORGOT TO ASK.

OF COURSE NOT. MEN LOVE A WOMAN WHO IS STRONG. IF HIS MALE EGO CAN'T HANDLE THAT, THEN HE'S NO GOOD FOR YOU.
DON'T LISTEN TO HIM, LUNA. JONAH FELT PROTECTIVE OF YOU. AND YOU MADE IT SEEM LIKE YOU DIDN'T NEED HIM. OF COURSE HE'S GOING TO BE HURT.
OH NO! YOU DIDN'T?
IS THAT BAD.
I TOLD HIM I COULD TAKE CARE OF MYSELF. I THINK HE WAS UPSET BY THAT.
WHAT SHOULD I DO?
OKAY, FIRST THING TOMORROW WE'RE GOING TO FIX THIS. YOU'LL TALK TO HIM. THANK HIM FOR LOOKING OUT FOR YOU.
MAYBE YOU SHOULD TELL HIM YOU WERE SO SCARED THAT YOU DON'T EVEN REALLY REMEMBER WHAT HAPPENED.
WILL THAT MAKE IT BETTER?
DEFINITELY.
I'M TELLING YOU, HE'S NOT WORTH IT.

FOLLOW ME!
I HEAR SOMETHING!
MAYBE THE JANITOR.
OLIVER, WHERE ARE WE GOING?
WE DON'T WANT TO GET CAUGHT. I KNOW ANOTHER WAY OUT.
WHAT'S THIS? IS SOMEONE ELSE DOWN HERE?

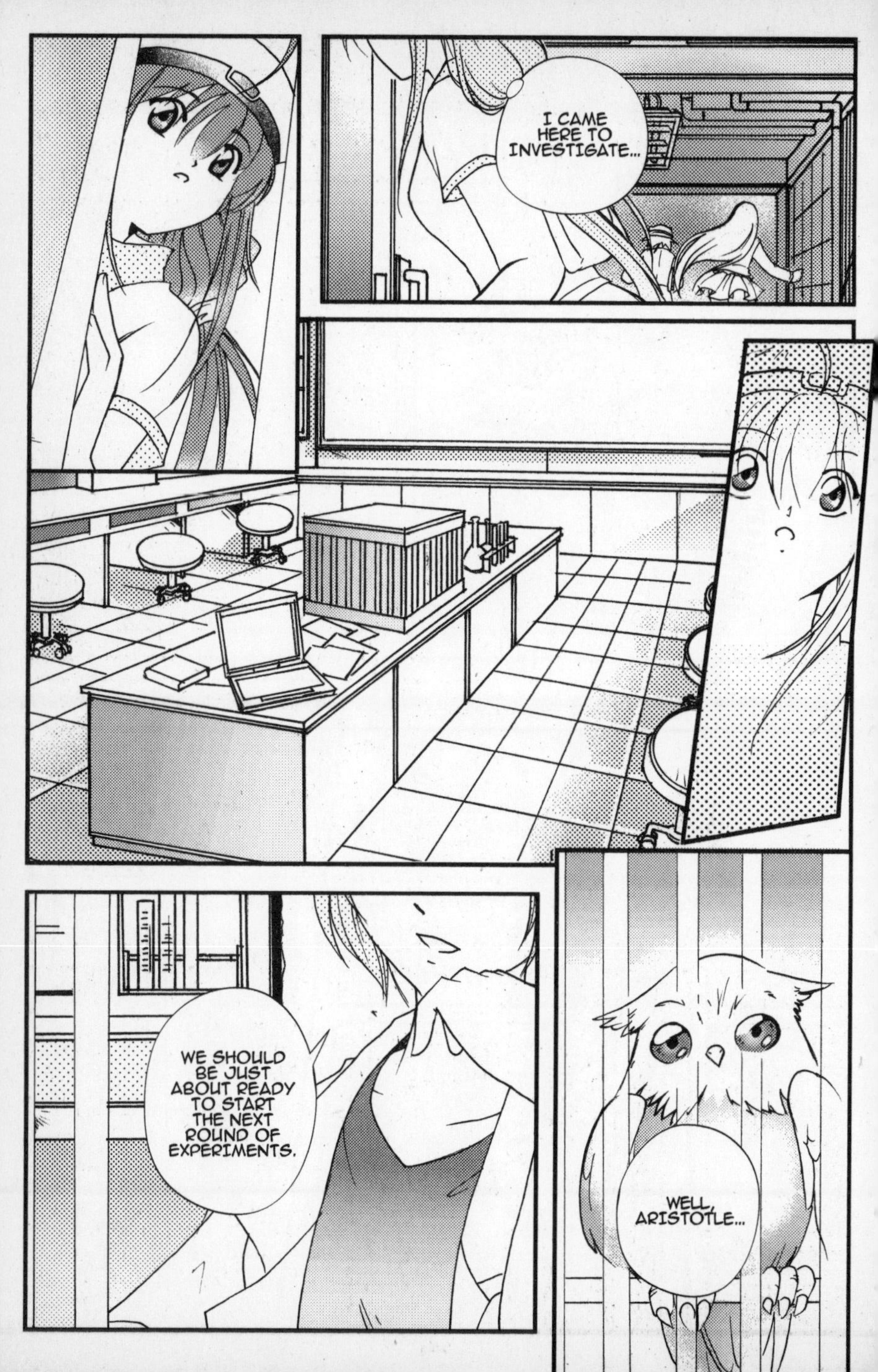
I CAME HERE TO INVESTIGATE...
WE SHOULD BE JUST ABOUT READY TO START THE NEXT ROUND OF EXPERIMENTS.
WELL, ARISTOTLE...

TODAY'S EXPERIMENT WAS A PARTIAL SUCCESS. WHILE MY STRENGTH-ENHANCING GENE THERAPY DOES WORK, THE OWLS WERE A BIT LARGER THAN THE ORIGINAL SPECIMEN.

UNACCEPTABLE! THEY MUST BE INDISTINGUISHABLE FROM THE ORIGINAL.

SUPER STRONG OWLS? WHAT'S VON BRUCKEN GOT PLANNED?

I THOUGHT I HEARD SOMETHING, BUT I WAS WRONG. LET'S GO.
NOTHING!
WHATCHA LOOKING AT?
I HAD HER!
I THINK I SHOULD TELL THEM THE TRUTH.
I COULD HAVE DONE SOMETHING BUT FRANCESCA AND OLIVER WERE THERE.

LUNA, CONSIDER WHAT A BIG THING THIS IS. YOU WERE BORN IN A LABORATORY AND RAISED TO BE A SPY. THAT'S A *LOT* TO TAKE IN.
YOU NEED TO BE SURE THEY'RE READY FOR THIS BEFORE YOU TELL THEM.

BEFORE? NO. THERE WILL BE *NO* TELLING. DO EITHER OF YOU KNOW THE MEANING OF '*TOP SECRET*'?

I JUST THOUGHT IT WOULD BE HELPFUL IF THEY KNEW. THEY'RE MY FRIENDS.
AND IT'S GOOD THAT YOU'RE MAKING FRIENDS. BUT--

NO BUTS. LUNA, YOU WILL TAKE YOUR STEALTH GEAR TO SCHOOL TOMORROW AND AFTER CLASS YOU WILL GO BACK TO THE LAB.
YOU WILL APPREHEND DR. WARREN AND GET OUT OF THERE BEFORE ANYONE CAN IDENTIFY YOU.
UNDERSTOOD?
YES, CONTROL.

I SHOULD USE FRANCESCA'S ADVICE.
I'LL TALK TO JONAH AND MAKE HIM LIKE ME AGAIN.
I THOUGHT MAYBE WE COULD GO SEE A MOVIE FRIDAY NIGHT.
A MOVIE? YEAH, SURE. WHY NOT?
I'M GONNA TAKE OUT DR. WARREN NOW. THE SOONER I'M OUT OF HERE, THE BETTER.
FINE. I DON'T CARE IF HE GOES OUT WITH HER. I DON'T BELONG HERE ANYWAY.

FINISHED

AMAZING ARTIST SHIEI

File 06
MISSION ACCOMPLISHED?

THERE GOES LUNA.
I WONDER WHAT'S BOTHERING HER?
MAY I HAVE A WORD WITH YOU, ELIZABETH?
OF COURSE.
ALONE.
GEEZ, FRANCESCA. RUDE MUCH?
ME RUDE? DON'T YOU KNOW THAT LUNA AND JONAH HAVE... WELL, HAVE SOMETHING GOING ON BETWEEN THEM?
AND TELL ME WHY I SHOULD CARE WHO THE NEW GIRL HAS A CRUSH ON? OR BETTER YET, WHY SHOULD YOU CARE?

SO? I CARE. BIG DEAL. SHE'S NICE.
ARE YOU SAYING I CAN'T BE FRIENDS WITH BOTH YOU AND LUNA?
SORRY, FRANCESCA. DOESN'T WORK THAT WAY. LOOK WHAT SHE'S DONE TO YOU. YOU'RE HANGING OUT WITH SKATEBOARD LOSERS NOW, TOO?

THAT'S EXACTLY WHAT I'M SAYING.

IT'S YOUR CHOICE.

SPIES DON'T CRY.

I DON'T CARE IF JONAH DOES HAVE BEAUTIFUL EYES.
I HAVE A JOB TO DO.
IF DR. WARREN IS DOWN HERE, I'LL TAKE CARE OF HER.
IF NOT, I'LL CLEAN OUT THE LAB AND FIND HER LATER.
AFTER ALL, I KNOW WHERE SHE'LL BE IN SECOND PERIOD.

LAB'S EMPTY. LET'S SEE WHAT EVIDENCE I CAN GET FOR CONTROL
BUT FIRST...
FLY FREE. GO. HURRY!
THERE YOU GO. C'MON, BOY.
DON'T BE AFRAID, ARISTOTLE.

SCREEECH!

WELL, WHAT DO WE HAVE HERE? A NINJA?

DAMN BIRD!

I'LL GET HIM BACK.

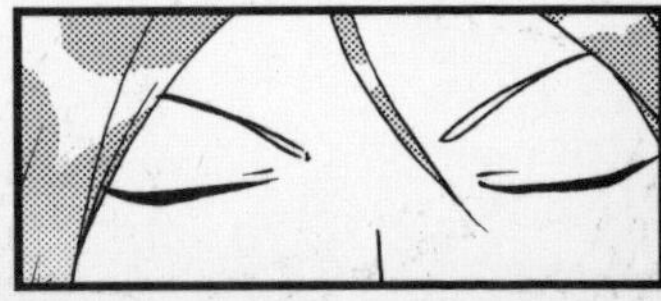

A NINJA VERSUS A SCIENCE TEACHER... IT HARDLY SEEMS **FAIR.**
AND IT ***ISN'T!***

BUT NOT IN THE WAY YOU THINK!
KICK
LET'S SEE WHAT YOU'VE GOT, CHILD!
UH-OH.

I GUESS IT WASN'T FAIR.
SO I'LL HAVE TO EVEN THE ODDS.
WHIP
SLASH
YIKES, SHE KNOWS HOW TO USE THAT.

THAT'S TAKEN THE FIGHT OUT OF YOU.
SNAG
REALLY KNOWS HOW TO USE THAT.
WHIP
WHIP
WHIP
WHIP
YOU LOOK YOUNG ENOUGH TO BE A STUDENT.
THIS IS BAD.
DR. WARREN! WHAT ARE YOU DOING?
GOOD BOY, ARISTOTLE, LEADING ME DOWN HERE.
NOW LET'S SEE WHO WE HAVE UNDER HERE.

KICK
SLAM!
MR. DREYFUS, HELP ME.
DON'T LET HER—
...GET AWAY.
IT WAS YOU?

I BROUGHT THE POLICE, MR. DREYFUS!
KIDNAPPING THE SCHOOL MASCOT IS A SERIOUS OFFENSE.
ARI! OH ARISTOTLE, THERE YOU ARE!
I THOUGHT WE WERE ALL FAMILY.
I'M VERY DISAPPOINTED IN YOU, DR. WARREN.

MY LOYALTY LIES WITH A DIFFERENT FAMILY.
WOW... DR. WARREN. MY MONEY WAS ON JONAH.
WE KNOW, OLIVER.
I'M JUST GLAD THEY CAUGHT HER.
LUNA! WHERE WERE YOU?
WE WERE WORRIED.

WELL, MAYBE HIGH SCHOOL ISN'T ALL BAD. I DID MAKE FRIENDS.
YOU TOLD HER SHE HAD TO CHOOSE?
LOOKS LIKE SHE DID.
WHATEVER. FRANCESCA IS SO YESTERDAY'S NEWS.
LET'S GO, GIRLS.

HEY, KNOW WHAT I HEARD? DR. WARREN TRIED TO CLONE ARISTOTLE.
EEWW! WHERE'D YOU HEAR THAT?

ARE YOU OKAY, FRANCESCA?
I'M FINE. WE SHOULD GO SHOPPING THIS WEEKEND.
ALRIGHT. THAT SOUNDS LIKE FUN.

THAT'S GROSS.
REALLY? WHY? I MEAN, IT'S WEIRD. BUT LIFE GROWN IN A LAB IS STILL LIFE.

PRINCIPAL OHLINGER WAS TALKING TO THE COPS. THEY FOUND ALL SORTS OF EVIDENCE IN THE LAB. THEY THINK THOSE OTHER OWLS WERE CLONES.

IT'S IMMORAL. IT'S WRONG. NOTHING GOOD CAN COME FROM IT.

THE AGENCY TOOK DR. WARREN OFF THE POLICE'S HANDS. GOOD WORK.
CONGRATULATIONS, LUNA.
OUR PEOPLE INTERVIEWED DR. WARREN. SHE DOESN'T KNOW WHAT THE COUNT WANTED WITH THE CLONED OWLS.
THANK YOU, CONTROL. SHOULD I PACK? ARE WE DONE HERE?
NOT YET, I'M AFRAID.
YOU WERE RIGHT, DR. ANDY. I CAN'T TELL THEM THE TRUTH. THEY WOULDN'T UNDERSTAND.
PLEASE DON'T MAKE ME GO BACK.
I THOUGHT YOU WERE MAKING FRIENDS.

I'M SORRY, LUNA. BUT VON BRUCKEN'S PLAN IS STILL A MYSTERY. YOU'LL REPORT BACK TO HIGH SCHOOL TOMORROW.
YES, YOU'RE SUCH A GOOD BOY.
!
THAT MUST HAVE BEEN SO TRAUMATIC FOR YOU, MY LITTLE ARI.

NO, GO AWAY, BIRD, I DON'T KNOW YOU.

I'M SERIOUS. WE'VE NEVER MET, OKAY!

FINE. BUT IT'S OUR *SECRET*.

GOOD MORNING, LUNA. MY, ARISTOTLE DOES SEEM TO LIKE YOU.

HE DOESN'T USUALLY RESPOND TO THE STUDENTS.

HE'S SWEET. I'D BETTER GET TO CLASS.

I WONDER WHO'S GOING TO TAKE DR. WARREN'S PLACE?
HEY, LUNA. NO TEACHER YET.
GOOD MORNING, CLASS.
I AM YOUR NEW SCIENCE TEACHER, PROFESSOR TROMPERIE.
I'M LOOKING FORWARD TO A VERY PRODUCTIVE YEAR.
THE MAN VON BRUCKEN HIRED IN PARIS.
IT'S HIM!

Welcome aboard the maiden voyage of the good ship we call Seven Seas.

There are many things we're trying to accomplish by publishing the book you're holding in your hands (or feet) right now, but first and foremost, we want to tell good stories. Like you, we read manga, and we love 'em. So when we started assembling a crew of fine artists and scurvy pirates to create original graphic novels, we never had to think twice about what kind of stories we wanted to tell. We knew it had to be manga.

Some of you may point out that the term manga means "comics from Japan." We've opted instead to use the term to describe a particular style of comics that we aspire to emulate. Like most manga fans, we know that manga is a lot more than characters with spiky hair and big eyes. There's a quality to manga that is hard to describe... it's artistically dynamic in a way that most American comics aren't. There's depth to the characters and to their relationships that we as readers are drawn to, there's a sense of action and pacing that is cinematic and compelling, and there's a uniquely wacky sense of humor – no one does chibi, or super-deformed characters, the way the Japanese do.

Until now, at least. You see, manga isn't just a Japanese artform anymore. It's enjoyed by millions of fans worldwide, and skilled manga creators are emerging across the globe, with their own unique stories to tell. Yes, Japan is the rightful birthplace of manga, but we are the New Frontier, we are the Manga Generation, we are...getting carried away? Ok, maybe. But when it comes right down to it, our goal is to create authentic manga as best we can, and not just because it's the hot new thing. But because it's a great way to tell stories. And because we're having so much fun doing it!

We hope you enjoy your first Seven Seas manga, and we encourage you to check out our other titles. Please do stop by our web site at www.gomanga.com and let us know what you think!

Best wishes from the crew at

Seven Seas

MANGA-FY ME!!

Congratulations to ***Christina George***, one of two Grand Prize winners in our Manga-fy Me Contest! Look for Christina's cameo on page 162 of this volume (hint: long plaid skirt.) And check out **gomanga.com** for more information on this and other exciting contests!

MEMORANDUM

TO: OUR READERS
FROM: NUNZIO DEFILIPPIS AND CHRISTINA WEIR
RE: AMAZING AGENT LUNA

Amazing Agent Luna is a true story.

Seriously.

We knew a girl in high school who was a secret agent. It took a while to figure it out, and she was very good at hiding it. But we could tell she was different because of the odd way she reacted to every little thing. We were also tipped off by the fact that whenever the bad guys attacked, she was never around, but 'someone' would always save the day. Then, when it was over, she'd be there, confused as ever.

She had never been in a social environment before and did she ever have a rough time. Everything was new for her, and she was unprepared for her emotions, for her first crushes, for her first love. She couldn't handle rejection, peer pressure, cliques, snobs, or any of the parts of high school that make it a singularly frustrating experience. But boy could she kick butt.

Okay, we lied. The girl we knew wasn't a secret agent. We didn't know anyone like Luna, because no-one is like Luna. We wanted to take a somewhat familiar concept - the complete innocent who is learning about the world - and tell the story from her point of view, instead of focusing on the people who find her, or befriend her (as many of those stories do). Luna gets to experience everything for the first time, and she gets to do it in high school.

But Luna isn't that unique. High school feels like alien terrain for all of us. Everything we encounter there is new and frustrating and confusing. And the cliques, the peer pressure, the snobs… they could drive anyone crazy, even if they weren't genetically engineered and raised in isolated government bases.

So Luna is everything a teenage girl must feel entering high school, only more. She's one step removed from anyone we know, but not so different that we don't want her to succeed in high school. Which is how we hope you'll react to her too.

But, unlike most teens, if all goes wrong for Luna, at least she can still kick butt.

Anyway, we hope you enjoy reading about Luna as much as we enjoyed writing about her. Seeing her come to life under Shiei's talented pencils has been an incredible thrill. If there is no-one in the world quite like Luna, it might be because of Shiei, who has turned our little girl into an Amazing Secret Agent.

CREATOR DOSSIER

WRITERS

Nunzio DeFilippis was born in New York, grew up in New York, loves New York, and lives in Los Angeles. He is a graduate of USC's screenwriting program and has written several feature films that no one will ever see, including one that was purchased by a production company that went out of business mere weeks later. After that, he started writing with Christina Weir.

Christina Weir was born in New York but spent her formative years in Boston. She has a Master's Degree in Television Production (for all the good that does) from Emerson College. She has lived in Los Angeles for the past ten years.

As a team, they have spent several years writing for television. They were on the writing staff of HBOs ARLISS for two seasons, and have worked on Disney's KIM POSSIBLE. In addition, they have written several feature films, none of which have been produced. This led them to explore the comics medium. Nunzio wrote an issue of DETECTIVE COMICS solo before collaborating with Christina on SKIN-WALKER for Oni Press. They have also written THREE STRIKES, MARIA'S WEDDING, THE TOMB and the ongoing fantasy story ONCE IN A BLUE MOON. Their work at Oni got the attention of Marvel Comics which led them to writing the relaunch of Marvel's teen mutant franchise NEW MUTANTS. This book has recently graduated to become NEW X-MEN: ACADEMY X. They've also written for DC Comics' WONDER WOMAN. Nunzio and Christina are married.

ARTIST

Shiei was grown in a laboratory some twenty odd years ago, bred from the finest artistic genes. She began drawing at an early age after learning how to hold a crayon and discovering what a good canvas stark white walls can make. She learned how to draw even better by sitting at her father's side, watching and helping him prepare visual aids for Shiei's school teacher mom. In her elementary school years, Shiei exhibited behavior that would forever alter the course of her life: she became hopelessly addicted to such tv anime as CANDY CANDY, SABER RIDERS, and DRAGON BALL Z.

In college, Shiei studied fine arts, with a major in advertising. She has never had a job in her entire life, unless you count babysitting her cousin. She currently lives in San Fernando Valley, with 11 parakeets, 6 cockatiels and 3 gold fish. When she grows up, Shiei would like to be a mad scientist.

Currently wants a Hachiko plushie

(Who's Hachiko? Check out BLADE FOR BARTER, another great Seven Seas title!)

PROJECT LUNA DF 1304-00

PROJECT LUNA
DESIGN FILES

HERE'S A SNEAK PEEK AT NUNZIO AND CHRISTINA'S VERY FIRST PROPOSAL FOR AMAZING AGENT LUNA. NOTICE HOW DIFFERENT THE TITLE WAS BACK THEN.

SUBJECT ORIGINAL PROPOSAL | SCOPE | TAB NO.

OPERATION: HIGHSCHOOL
A proposal for an original manga series
By Nunzio DeFilippis & Christina Weir

Operation: Highschool (name subject to change in case it's in use) is the story of Luna, the perfect secret agent. A girl grown in a lab from the finest genetic material, she has been trained since her birth fifteen years ago to be the United States government's ultimate espionage weapon. But she will get an assignment that will test her to the utmost of her capacity – high school.

Luna has just defeated the evil Count Von Brucken, but his lab makes it clear something big and scary will be going down at Nobel High, the elite high school maintained by the U.N. for the children of diplomats, scientists and other international figures. This master plan is unspecified and will come down by graduation day for the class of 2007. Needing an agent who can work undercover at a high school, the government sends in Luna.

But the one thing Luna has not been trained to handle is her own feelings. They are powerful and out of control, your average teen, but without parents or real interaction to steer her. And worse, no one ever thought she'd need to figure them out. Putting her in high school is lighting the fuse on an emotional bomb of adolescent confusion. Especially when she starts to make friends, and have crushes, including a flirtation with Jonah, the son of Von Brucken.

ON THE FOLLOWING PAGES YOU'LL FIND N & C'S EARLY NOTES ON THE CAST AND SHIEI'S CHARACTER DESIGNS. CAN YOU DETECT ALL THE CHANGES TO THE FINAL DESIGN AND STORYLINE?

Character sketches - LUNA

PORT PRODUCED AT	DATE PRODUCED	FILE PROCESSED BY	NATURE OF REPORT	FILE NO.
CHQ D-6			[CLASSIFIED]	

SUBJECT ORIGINAL LUNA PROFILE	SCOPE	TAB NO.

Luna is the perfect girl. She's smart, she's strong, she's agile, she's attractive. But for a secret agent, she is a complete innocent. Luna was never allowed to be a child, spending her early years learning and training with adult agents. She is expected to be emotion free as a result, but instead, adolescence has brought all the turmoil one would expect from a teen crashing to the surface. It's lingering just under the surface until she gets assigned to Nobel High. And then it explodes. When she first arrives, her cover is that she's from the country. So she dresses as a bumpkin – in overalls, etc. Once she makes friends, she'll get a makeover to be more of a city girl. But she'll never lose that cute innocence that somehow makes her even more attractive.

PROJECT LUNA DF 1304-00

Character sketches - LUNA

FILE NO.

REPORT PRODUCED AT	DATE PRODUCED	FILE PROCESSED BY	NATURE OF REPORT
CHQ D-6			[CLASSIFIED]

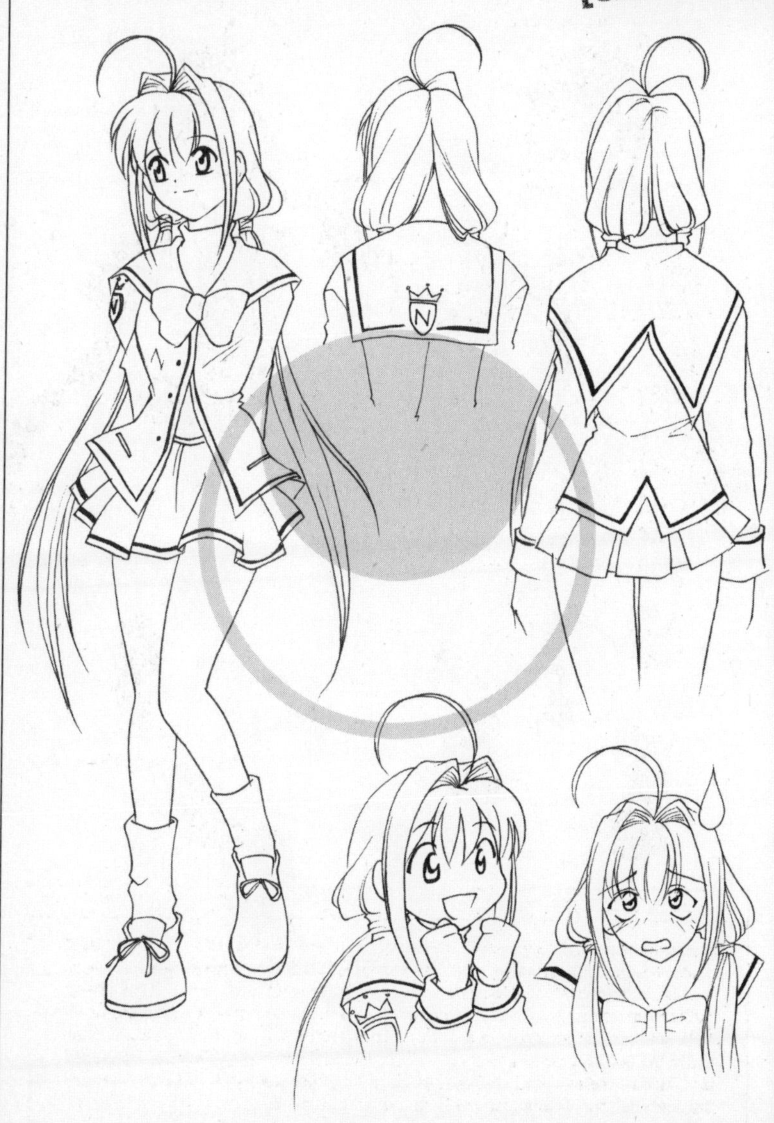

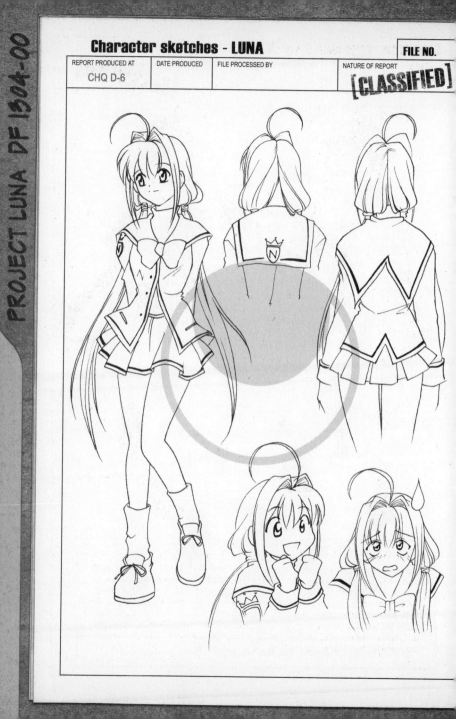

Character sketches - COUNT HEINRICH VON BRUCKEN

FILE NO.			
REPORT PRODUCED AT	DATE PRODUCED	FILE PROCESSED BY	NATURE OF REPORT
CHQ D-6			[CLASSIFIED]

SUBJECT ADDENDUM	SCOPE	TAB NO.
Early Von Brucken designs looked like a cross between Doctor Strange and Count Dracula.		

PROJECT LUNA DF 1504-00

Character sketches - COUNT HEINRICH VON BRUCKEN

FILE NO.			
REPORT PRODUCED AT	DATE PRODUCED	FILE PROCESSED BY	NATURE OF REPORT
CHQ D-6			[CLASSIFIED]

SUBJECT ORIGINAL VON BRUCKEN PROFILE	SCOPE	TAB NO.

Our bad guy. Count Von Brucken is a Count from the small Eastern European nation of Bruckenwald. Never heard of Bruckenwald? That's because it is basically a mountaintop in Eastern Europe - one castle ruled by the Count with an iron fist. He wants to bring the whole world under his control, but after the beginning of our story, he is in jail as a result of Luna's actions – though he never sees her face. His master plan centers on Nobel High, but no one knows why. He is evil, but like his son, there is a roguish good look to him. He's in his forties, strong and powerful. He carries himself like a king.

Character sketches - JONAH VON BRUCKEN

FILE NO.			
REPORT PRODUCED AT	DATE PRODUCED	FILE PROCESSED BY	NATURE OF REPORT
CHQ D-6			[CLASSIFIED]

SUBJECT	SCOPE	TAB NO.
ORIGINAL JONAH PROFILE		

Jonah is the handsome, mysterious brooder, equally new to Nobel High. His connection to Count Von Brucken will make him number one suspect in whatever the Count's evil plans are. But Jonah's affiliation will remain a mystery up til the end. Jonah is the type to wear a long coat and stand alone in the moonlight. In short, he's the dangerous loner that high school girls shouldn't like, but always do. His arrival at Nobel High will have all the girls swooning.

PROJECT LUNA DF 1304-00

Character sketches - OLIVER RIGGS

FILE NO.

REPORT PRODUCED AT	DATE PRODUCED	FILE PROCESSED BY	NATURE OF REPORT
CHQ D-6			[CLASSIFIED]

SUBJECT ORIGINAL OLIVER PROFILE	SCOPE	TAB NO.

Oliver is the underachiever son of one of the Security personnel who keeps tabs on the United Nations. A lot of the other kids give Oliver grief because his parents aren't diplomats or geniuses. Some give him grief because he's a little dorky at times. But Oliver is reliable, good natured and a fast friend to Luna. Oliver should have that boy next door quality. While his father is a towering hulk of a man, Oliver should be pretty unremarkable in physique. Picture Oliver as the skateboarding, picked on type. He's too much fun for the dorks, and too odd for the in crowd.

Character sketches - ELIZABETH WESTBROOK

FILE NO.			
PORT PRODUCED AT	DATE PRODUCED	FILE PROCESSED BY	NATURE OF REPORT
CHQ D-6			[CLASSIFIED]

SUBJECT ORIGINAL ELIZABETH PROFILE	SCOPE	TAB NO.

Elizabeth is a snooty English girl, the daughter of UN diplomat and a brillant scientist. Elizabeth is smart, beautiful and popular and she knows it. She is the stuck-up foil for Luna. Francesca and Elizabeth start out as friends but have a falling out when Francesca befriends Luna, and starts hanging out with Luna and Oliver. She's the kind of girl who hems her school skirt so short that it's practically a belt. Elizabeth loves to look good and that should be key to her look. Elizabeth is blonde.

PROJECT LUNA DF 1504-00

Character sketches - FRANCESCA ALDANA

REPORT PRODUCED AT	DATE PRODUCED	FILE PROCESSED BY	NATURE OF REPORT	FILE NO.
CHQ D-6			[CLASSIFIED]	

SUBJECT ORIGINAL FRANCESCA PROFILE	SCOPE	TAB NO.

Francesca is the fifteen year old daughter of Spanish diplomats. She is all grace and charm. She runs with the beautiful people crowd of high school, but isn't as stuck-up. She's the one who takes Luna on as a project for a makeover to try to get her in with the cool kids. When the cool kids continue to reject Luna, Francesca will have to make a choice. Francesca is hip, precociously sexy and always dressed in the latest fashion with long flowy hair.

Character sketches - "CONTROL"/AGENT JENNIFER KAJIWARA

ORT PRODUCED AT	DATE PRODUCED	FILE PROCESSED BY	NATURE OF REPORT	FILE NO.
CHQ D-6			[CLASSIFIED]	

SUBJECT ORIGINAL CONTROL PROFILE	SCOPE	TAB NO.

Luna's by the book, hard as nails Control Agent. Jennifer is the daughter of a Japanese businessman and a American writer. Jennifer left home after college and never returned, disappearing into the mystery life of a secret agent. She gets a new assignment when Luna does. She'll remain a control agent, but with a new codename: Mom. Jennifer is in her mid-thirties, uptight, by the book and a little too sterile. She should be a variation on the sexy librarian. Glasses, very businesslike and probably quite the hottie if she ever let her hair down.

PROJECT LUNA DF 1304-00

Character sketches - DR. ANDY COLLINS

REPORT PRODUCED AT	DATE PRODUCED	FILE PROCESSED BY	NATURE OF REPORT	FILE NO.
CHQ D-6			[CLASSIFIED]	

SUBJECT ORIGINAL DR. ANDY PROFILE	SCOPE	TAB NO.

The government psychiatrist assigned to keep an eye on Luna when she hits her teen years. He's been saying all along that Luna needs training with her emotions, but Control never listened to him. Now that Luna's been assigned to High School, Dr. Andy will get re-assigned. He will play Luna's Dad, opposite Control, who he really can't stand. Dr. Andy is in his forties, laid back, good natured. A feel good kind of guy with a ponytail and an earring. He will love playing "Dad" to Luna because he thinks she really needs it.

[FOR YOUR EYES ONLY]

BEHIND THE SCENES

Making manga's a lot like making movies. First you start with a screenplay. Then you make storyboards based on that screenplay. The final art is then created based on the storyboards.

Let's a take an inside look at the first couple pages of Nunzio and Christina's script, and see how it was translated by Shiei into ruffs.

CHAPTER 1: AMAZING AGENT
EXT. PARIS, FRANCE NIGHT
WE OPEN ON THE PARIS SKYLINE, DOMINATED BY THE EIFFEL TOWER.
THEN WE CUT TO ONE OF PARIS' BEAUTIFUL STREETS BEFORE SETTLING ON:
EXT. BRUCKENSTEIN EMBASSY, PARIS - NIGHT
THE EMBASSY FOR THE NATION OF BRUCKENSTEIN. A SIGN HANGS ON THE WROUGHT IRON FENCE THAT SURROUNDS THE BUILDING. THE SIGN READS: L'AMBASSADE DE BRUCKENSTEIN. UNDERNEATH, IN ENGLISH IT SAYS: BRUCKENSTEIN EMBASSY.
L'AMBASSADE DE BRUCKEN
EMBASSY
ARDS WITH MACHINE GUNS STAND OUT FRONT. THEY ARE DRESSED IN ANDARD MILITARY GARB AND WEAR BERETS. THE BUILDING ITSELF IS IN E MIDDLE OF THE BLOCK, BUT IS ISOLATED. NONE OF THE NEARBY ILDINGS ARE EVEN REMOTELY CLOSE TO IT.
TEENAGE GIRL WALKS PAST THE EMBASSY, LOOKING UP AT IT'S ROOF. T'S LUNA, IN JEANS AND A SWEATER WITH A BACKPACK OVER HER HOULDER.
XT. SIDEWALK CAFE - SAME
JUST DOWN THE BLOCK FROM THE EMBASSY IS A TYPICAL PARISIAN CAFE. SEATED AT ONE OF THE TABLES, DRINKING COFFEE, IS JONAH. HE IS DRESSED IN HIS TRENCHCOAT AND IS BROODY AND HANDSOME. HE SMILES AND WE CAN SEE HE'S WATCHING LUNA AS SHE COMES WALKING DOWN THE STREET.
LUNA LOOKS LIKE YOUR AVERAGE FIFTEEN YEAR OLD GIRL. NOTHING ABOUT HER JUMPS OUT THOUGH. SHE'S DRESSED CASUALLY, BUT SHE IS QUITE ATTRACTIVE.
JONAH
HELLO.. WHAT HAVE WE HERE?
HELLO...
...WHAT HAVE WE HERE
rns into the alley an
ead, mystified, and w
covering her face. W
ilding.
Luna attaches
Down below, t
INT. VON BRU
COUNT VON B
Von Brucken s
VON BRUCKE
are you i

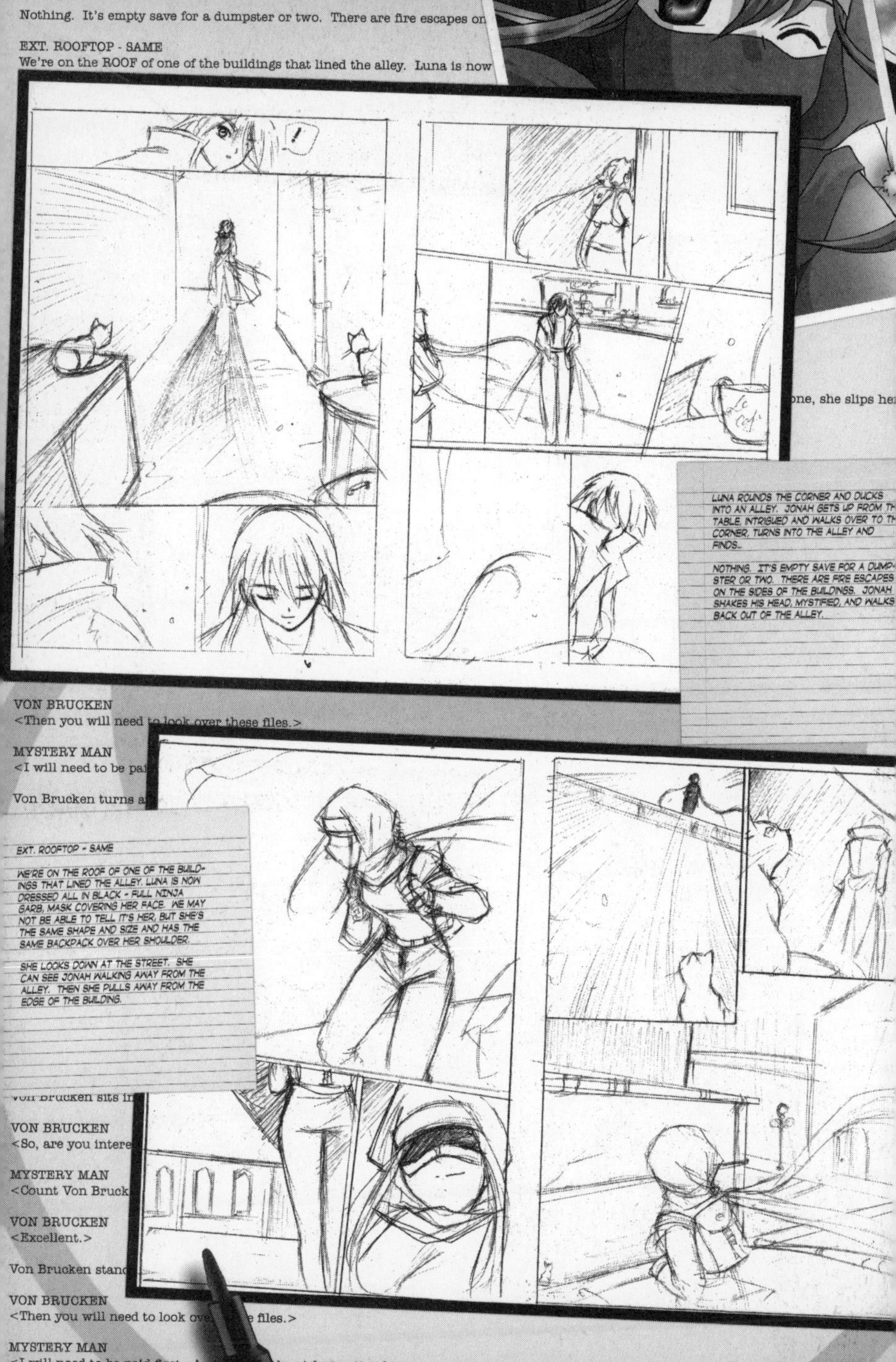

Nothing. It's empty save for a dumpster or two. There are fire escapes on
EXT. ROOFTOP - SAME
We're on the ROOF of one of the buildings that lined the alley. Luna is now
one, she slips he
LUNA ROUNDS THE CORNER AND DUCKS INTO AN ALLEY. JONAH GETS UP FROM TH TABLE, INTRIGUED AND WALKS OVER TO TH CORNER, TURNS INTO THE ALLEY AND FINDS...
NOTHING. IT'S EMPTY SAVE FOR A DUMP-STER OR TWO. THERE ARE FIRE ESCAPES ON THE SIDES OF THE BUILDINGS. JONAH SHAKES HIS HEAD, MYSTIFIED, AND WALKS BACK OUT OF THE ALLEY.
VON BRUCKEN
<Then you will need to look over these files.>
MYSTERY MAN
<I will need to be pa
Von Brucken turns a
EXT. ROOFTOP - SAME
WE'RE ON THE ROOF OF ONE OF THE BUILD-INGS THAT LINED THE ALLEY. LUNA IS NOW DRESSED ALL IN BLACK - FULL NINJA GARB, MASK COVERING HER FACE. WE MAY NOT BE ABLE TO TELL IT'S HER, BUT SHE'S THE SAME SHAPE AND SIZE AND HAS THE SAME BACKPACK OVER HER SHOULDER.
SHE LOOKS DOWN AT THE STREET. SHE CAN SEE JONAH WALKING AWAY FROM THE ALLEY. THEN SHE PULLS AWAY FROM THE EDGE OF THE BUILDING.
VON BRUCKEN
<So, are you intere
MYSTERY MAN
<Count Von Bruck
VON BRUCKEN
<Excellent.>
Von Brucken stand
VON BRUCKEN
<Then you will need to look ov e files.>
MYSTERY MAN
<I will need to be paid first. And her jobs to attend to.>

human could make this jump. Then she backs up, breaks into a run and LE
clears the dis
n below, the
a moves to a
a attaches a s
n below, the d
VON BRUCK
NT VON BRU
Brucken sits
N BRUCKEN
are you inter
SHE WALKS ACROSS THE ROOF AND SIZES UP THE GAP BETWEEN THIS BUILDING AND THE EMBASSY. NO HUMAN COULD MAKE THIS JUMP. THEN SHE BACKS UP, BREAKS INTO A RUN AND LEAPS. SHE CLEARS THE DISTANCE EASILY, AND LANDS WITHOUT A SOUND ONTO THE EMBASSY ROOF.
DOWN BELOW, THE GUARDS STAND WITH THEIR GUNS, UNAWARE. LUNA MOVES TO A SKYLIGHT ON THE ROOF. SHE PEERS THROUGH IT INTO AN ORNATELY DECORATED OFFICE BELOW. THERE IS NO ONE THERE.
one, she slips her han
He is followed in by
y Man stands in fro
will need to be paid first. And I have other jobs to attend to.>
n Brucken turns away from the cabinet, swishing his cape again - he LOVES to do that. Up above, I

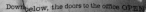

around it with a glass cutter, lifting a small circle of glass out. Once done, she slips her

Down below, the doors to the office OPEN

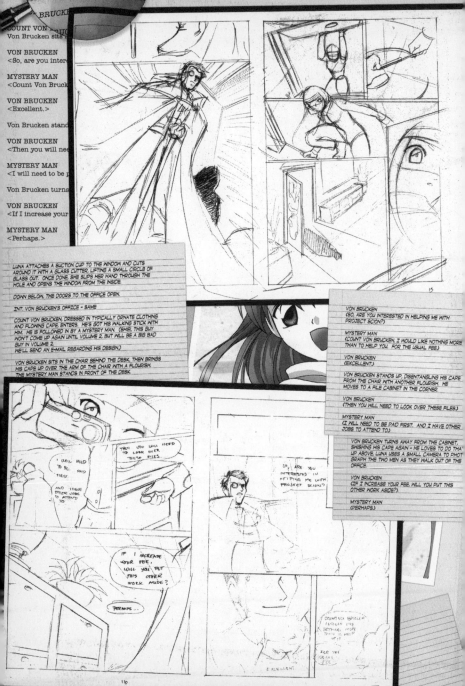

BRUCKE

COUNT VON

Von Brucken sits

VON BRUCKEN

<So, are you intere

MYSTERY MAN

<Count Von Bruck

VON BRUCKEN

<Excellent.>

Von Brucken stand

VON BRUCKEN

<Then you will nee

MYSTERY MAN

<I will need to be p

Von Brucken turns

VON BRUCKEN

<If I increase your

MYSTERY MAN

<Perhaps.>

LUNA ATTACHES A SUCTION CUP TO THE WINDOW AND CUTS AROUND IT WITH A GLASS CUTTER, LIFTING A SMALL CIRCLE OF GLASS OUT. ONCE DONE, SHE SLIPS HER HAND THROUGH THE HOLE AND OPENS THE WINDOW FROM THE INSIDE.

DOWN BELOW, THE DOORS TO THE OFFICE OPEN.

INT. VON BRUCKEN'S OFFICE - SAME

COUNT VON BRUCKEN, DRESSED IN TYPICALLY ORNATE CLOTHING AND FLOWING CAPE, ENTERS. HE'S GOT HIS WALKING STICK WITH HIM. HE IS FOLLOWED IN BY A MYSTERY MAN. (SHIEI, THIS GUY WON'T COME UP AGAIN UNTIL VOLUME 2, BUT WILL BE A BIG BAD GUY IN VOLUME 2.
WE'LL SEND AN E-MAIL REGARDING HIS DESIGN.)

VON BRUCKEN SITS IN THE CHAIR BEHIND THE DESK, THEN BRINGS HIS CAPE UP OVER THE ARM OF THE CHAIR WITH A FLOURISH. THE MYSTERY MAN STANDS IN FRONT OF THE DESK.

VON BRUCKEN
(SO, ARE YOU INTERESTED IN HELPING ME WITH PROJECT SCION?)

MYSTERY MAN
(COUNT VON BRUCKEN, I WOULD LIKE NOTHING MORE THAN TO HELP YOU. FOR THE USUAL FEE.)

VON BRUCKEN
(EXCELLENT.)

VON BRUCKEN STANDS UP, DISENTANGLING HIS CAPE FROM THE CHAIR WITH ANOTHER FLOURISH. HE MOVES TO A FILE CABINET IN THE CORNER.

VON BRUCKEN
(THEN YOU WILL NEED TO LOOK OVER THESE FILES.)

MYSTERY MAN
(I WILL NEED TO BE PAID FIRST. AND I HAVE OTHER JOBS TO ATTEND TO.)

VON BRUCKEN TURNS AWAY FROM THE CABINET, SWISHING HIS CAPE AGAIN - HE LOVES TO DO THA UP ABOVE, LUNA USES A SMALL CAMERA TO PHOT GRAPH THE TWO MEN AS THEY WALK OUT OF THE OFFICE.

VON BRUCKEN
(IF I INCREASE YOUR FEE, WILL YOU PUT THIS OTHER WORK ASIDE?)

MYSTERY MAN
(PERHAPS.)

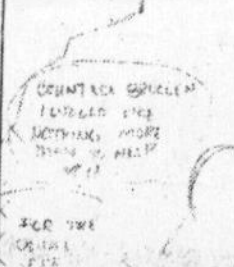

Nunzio DeFilippis | Christina Weir | Shiei

Luna's undercover work at Nobel High gets more dangerous, with the coming of the new Science teacher – a known agent of Count Von Brucken! But Luna's problems don't stop there – her friends are on the verge of discovering her secrets, and Jonah, the brooding boy of her dreams, begins dating snobbish Elizabeth, who's made it her personal mission to make Luna's life miserable.

Look for it in June 2005!

Seven Seas

NEW WORLDS AT YOUR FINGERTIPS
www.gomanga.com

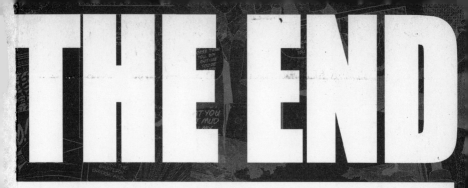

THE END

YOU'RE READING THE WRONG WAY

This is the last page of
Amazing Agent Luna Volume 1.

This book reads from right to left, Japanese style. To read from the beginning, flip the book over to the other side, start with the top right panel, and take it from there.

If this is your first time reading manga, just follow the diagram. It may seem backwards at first, but you'll get used to it! Have fun!